Adventures on Wisconsin's Ice Age Trail

Day Hikes, Weekend Jaunts, and Family Vacations

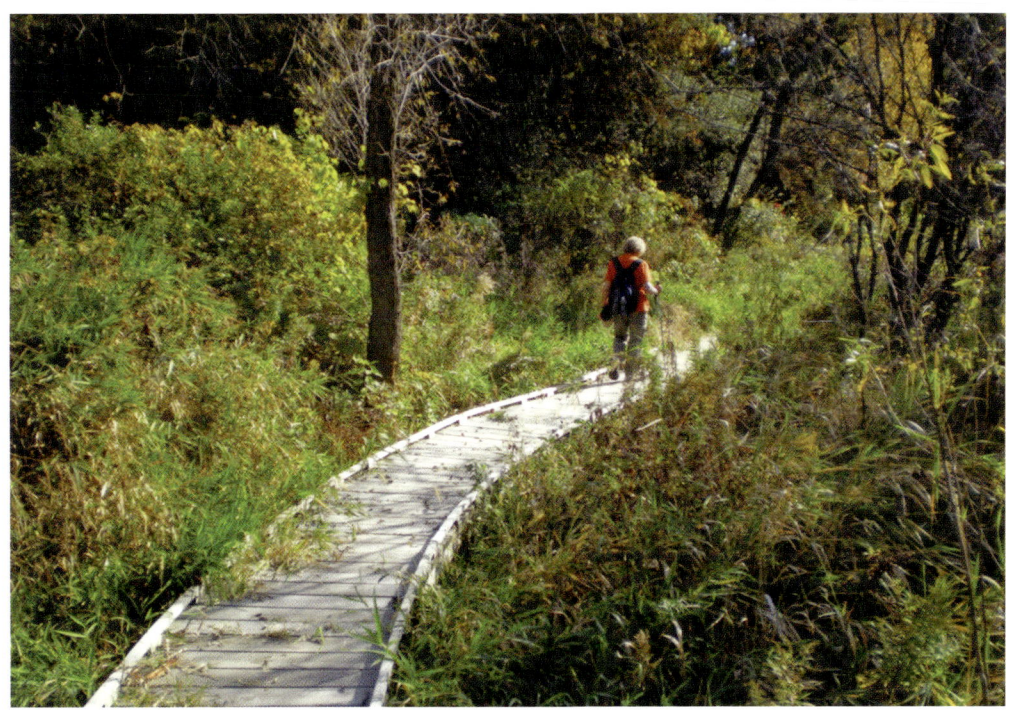

By Sylvia Oberle and Kristine Rued-Clark

All photographs by Sylvia Oberle except where noted

Foreword by Congressman David R. Obey

Book design by Cody Popp

Published by Capitol Cat Press

Printed by Worzalla Publishing, Stevens Point, Wisconsin

Happy Trails!
Sylvia Oberle

Copyright © 2015 by Capitol Cat Press

All rights reserved. No part of this publication may be reproduced, distributed, or transmitted in any form or by any means, including photocopying, recording, or other electronic or mechanical methods, without the prior written permission of the publisher, except in the case of brief quotations embodied in critical reviews and certain other noncommercial uses permitted by copyright law. For permission requests, write to the publisher, addressed "Attention: Permission Coordinator," at the address below.

Capitol Cat Press
N 14175 Koser Avenue
Stanley, Wisconsin 54768

Ordering Information:
Quantity sales. Special discounts are available on quantity purchases by corporations, associations, and others. For details, contact the publisher at the address above or by emailing capitolcatpress@centurytel.net.

Printed in the United States of America
Book and cover design by Cody Popp, Waupaca, Wisconsin

Publisher's Cataloging-in-Publication data

Oberle, Sylvia.
Adventures on Wisconsin's Ice Age Trail : Day Hikes , Weekend Jaunts , and Family Vacations / by Sylvia Oberle and Kristine Rued-Clark.
pages cm.
ISBN 978-0-692-48306-0
Includes index.

1. Walking –Wisconsin –Guidebooks. 2. Trails –Wisconsin –Guidebooks.
3. Wisconsin –Guidebooks. 4. Hiking –Wisconsin. I. Rued-Clark, Kristine. II. Title.

F579.3 .O24 2015
917.7504/43 –dc23   Library of Congress control number: 2015947688
Several of Sylvia Oberle's essays were previously published, in a slightly different form, in the *Washburn County Register* and are reprinted here with permission.
The poem, "October on the Ice Age Trail," by Kristine Rued-Clark, appeared in Verse & Vision II, A Collaboration of Poetry and Arts, © 2012 by Q Artists Cooperative, and is reprinted here with permission.
Sylvia Oberle's photograph of David R. Obey first appeared on the jacket of his book, *Raising Hell for Justice, The Washington Battles of a Heartland Progressive*, published by The University of Wisconsin Press, © 2007, and is reprinted here with permission.

The individual authors and photographers retain all rights to their work.

First Edition, 2015

ISBN 978-0-692-48306-0

To my husband, Gene, and daughter, Marie
– Sylvia

For Steve with gratitude for all his encouragement
– Kris

Table of Contents

Foreword – Congressman David R. Obey 7
Preface 9
"Mistress of the Ice Age Trail" – Richard Korb 11
Introduction 14
Tenderfoot Hiker – Superior Lobe 18
St. Croix Falls Segment (including Gandy Dancer Segment) –
Polk County (Maps 1, 2 & 3f) 21
Smile and "Bear" It 24
Hikes for Tree Lovers and Tree Huggers 25
Woodland Wonder 27
"Ode to Autumn Trees" 30
Pine Lake & Straight River Segments – Polk County (Maps 3 & 4f) 32
Once in a Blue Moon 34
Superior Lobe (including Hemlock Creek & Tuscobia Trail Segments) –
Barron & Washburn Counties (Maps 6-10f) 35
Chippewa Moraine Segment – Chippewa County (Map 15f) 41
Ice Age Trail Adventure -- Chippewa Moraine 46
Mondeaux Esker Segment – Taylor County (Map 23f) 48
Mondeaux Esker 50
"September Hike" 51
Grandfather Falls Segment – Lincoln County (Map 28f) 52
September Journey
Wisconsin's Northwoods along the Wisconsin River 54
"October on the Ice Age Trail" 55
Eau Claire Dells Segment – Marathon County (Maps 40 & 41f) 58
Ice Age Trail Adventure-- Eau Claire Dells 60
"You Go Ahead, I'll Wait" 62
Belmont, Emmons & Hartman Creek Segments –
Portage & Waupaca Counties (Map 48f) 63
Meeting Chapter Members
Hike-A-Thon Welcomes Visitors for Fall Colors 64
"January on the Ice Age Trail" 68
A New Angle 70
Spring Morning and the Mourning Cloak 71

Deerfield Segment – Waushara County (Map 50f) 72
Portage Canal Segment - Columbia & Sauk Counties (Maps 57 & 58f) 73
Walking through Portage 76
Devil's Lake Segment – Sauk County (Map 61f) 77
Those Vipers 81
"Turkey Vultures on Spirit Lake" 82
Cranes: Least and Most in Wisconsin 83
Restored Prairie - Dane County (Map 67f) 85
Restored Prairie – Columbia & Dane County 86
Lapham Peak Segment – Waukesha County (Maps 81 & 82f) 87
Increase Miles on the Ice Age Trail 88
"Spring on the Kettle Moraine" 91
Southern Holy Hill Segment, Washington County (Maps 83-84f) 93
"Towers and Spires" 95
Climb a Tower for Color 96
Thanks to Dad: I Love Rocks 98
"Manitowoc" 102
The Ice Age Trail
On and Near Rustic Roads–
(Kewaunee & Manitowoc Counties) (Maps 95-101f) 103
Road Walk on the IAT
Variety, Spice for a Walk 105
"Ice Age Trail, Maplewood" 107
Sturgeon Bay Segment – Eastern Terminus - Door County (Maps 104 & 105f) 108
Meeting Jason Dorgan
A Door County Ice Age Trail Adventure 110
One More Tower 112
"Thanks, Coach" 117
Ice Age National Scenic Trail Map 118
Acknowledgments 119
About the Authors 122
Wanderer's Haiku 125
Photo Index 126

Foreword

Wisconsin's Ice Age Trail calls to residents and visitors to get outdoors, stretch their legs, breathe clean air, and enjoy the scenery as they go. Hiking the trail is a time and place to enjoy nature as well as observe Wisconsin's many geological formations. Hikers will see a variety of moraines, drumlins, eskers, and kettle lakes. The trail meanders over 1,200 miles, outlining the farthest reach of the last glacier that advanced ten thousand years ago. It provides a wonderful low cost way for families to enjoy the outdoors and learn about Wisconsin geological history at the same time.

When I served in the United States House of Representatives, my district encompassed nine of the twenty-one Ice Age Trail chapters, more than any other congressional district in Wisconsin. I have good memories of working with the Ice Age Park and Trail Foundation (now renamed as the Ice Age Trail Alliance), the National Park Service, Land and Water Conservation Fund, Wisconsin DNR, and Wisconsin Forestry Service to provide federal support as a member of the House of Representatives from Wisconsin. I am also proud of my work helping obtain funds for the visitor center on the Chippewa Moraine. Civic and youth organizations, individual volunteers, and private landowners all work together to provide us with this beautiful trail. It has been a truly bipartisan effort to preserve this great legacy.

The natural beauty of our state is a legacy we all cherish. Back in 1958 Ray Zillmer worked with other organizers to create a national park. It was their desire to protect the geological features that were formed when the glacier retreated from Wisconsin at the end of the last Ice Age. It's difficult to live in Wisconsin without being a conservationist, and many of Wisconsin's senators and representatives have fit that description. Representative Henry Reuss was instrumental in forming the Ice Age National Scientific Reserve, giving special status to nine geologic gems across Wisconsin. The intent was for the Ice Age Trail to connect these gems. In 1980 the Ice Age Trail was designated by Congress as part of the National Scenic Trails System.

Most people today know of Earth Day, but not nearly as many know that Wisconsin's Senator Gaylord Nelson founded Earth Day. He also believed in protecting land for the benefit of the public. The Western Terminus of the Ice Age Trail is dedicated to Senator Gaylord Nelson. Representative Henry Reuss, Senator Gaylord Nelson, and many other Legislators and Governors were the driving force behind this unusual type of National Park, a hiking trail.

Just as I am proud to call Wisconsin my home state, I am proud to call the Ice Age Trail part of my legacy. It is the legacy of all those who have worked hard to create and maintain this trail that so beautifully showcases the natural wonders of our state. I have many pleasant memories of hiking on the Trail and I am proud, too, that throughout the history of the Ice Age Trail, helping to build it and maintain it has been a bipartisan effort. I encourage you to visit this wonderful trail for exercise and fun with your family and friends. Take time for at least a day's walk on the Ice Age Trail. The scenery will amaze you.

– Congressman David R. Obey

Preface

"You have to live for me now, Mother. Finish the trail for Daddy and me." Those were the words of my beautiful daughter Marie, who died of breast cancer July 1, 2010. So that is what I vowed to do. Finish all 1,000 miles of the Ice Age Trail. At that point, I had finished 780 miles of the trail.

Walking the trail gave me a reason to keep going. Not only was I grieving the loss of Marie, but also I was sadly missing my driver, my dear husband Gene, who passed away a month before our daughter. So many times he would drop me off and then pick me up seven to ten miles farther where a road crossed the Ice Age Trail. He loved seeing Wisconsin and the formations the glacier left. After I'd completed a hike, he'd say, "You have to see this rustic road!" And off we'd go to see some more of our beautiful state.

This book is the story of my adventures on the Ice Age Trail, along with my friend, Kris Rued-Clark, who walked many miles with me. We have highlighted some of our favorite segments in hopes that you, too, will explore the trail and create your own adventures, with friends, family, and those you may meet on chapter hikes.

– Sylvia

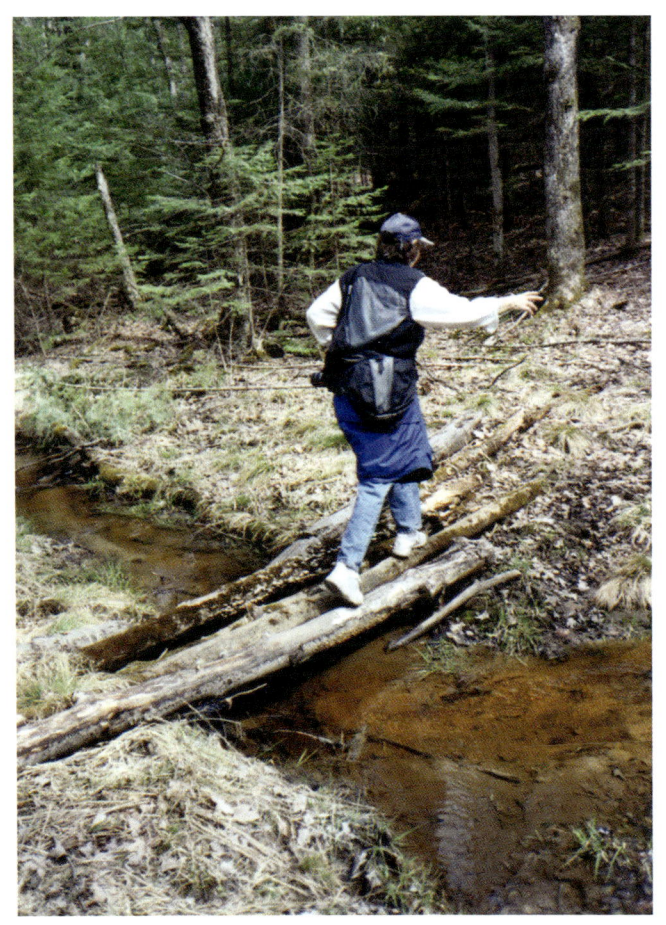

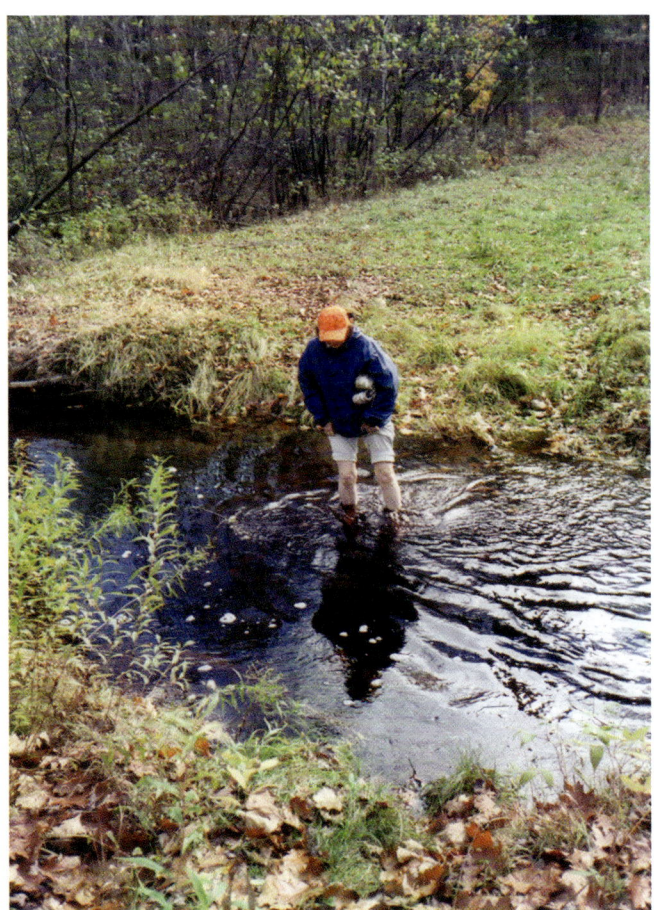

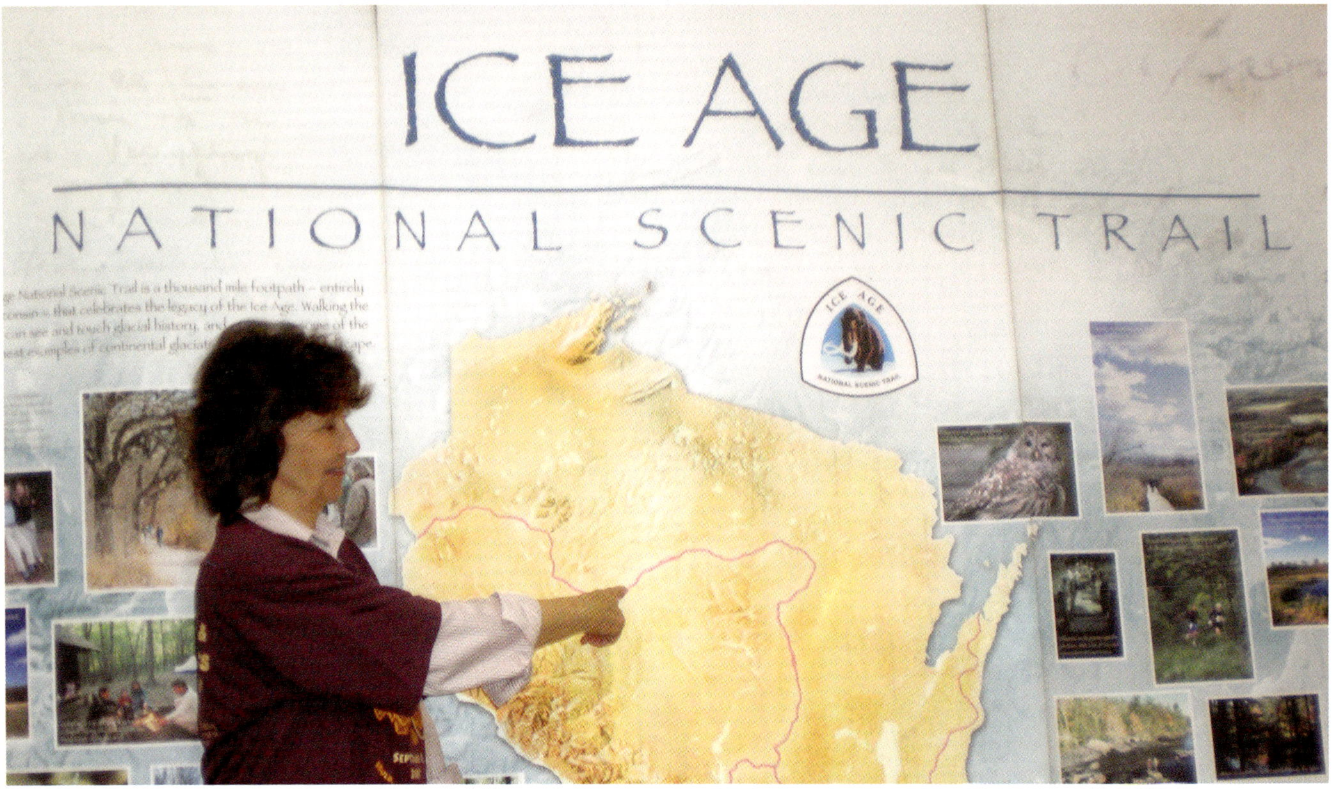
ICE AGE
NATIONAL SCENIC TRAIL
ICE AGE
NATIONAL SCENIC TRAIL

Mistress of the Ice Age Trail

She who walks the Ice Age Trail
Searching for the Holy Grail
She knows not what the future brings
Cares only for the natural things.

As she walks in solitude
The birds and trees observe the interlude.
Too busy with their daily rounds
They allow her passage on their grounds.

Though she walks by night and day
In her sleep she knows the way.
The trail is long, the hills are steep,
But the quest is a promise to keep.
The pleasure of the natural things
Is the walker's silent wings.
Once covered by a mass of ice,
The trail abounds with nature's life.
The journey is long, but not in vain.
A promise kept is a future gain.
The world will little note her passing there.
Only the birds and trees her passage share.

– Richard Korb

Introduction

Eskers, kames, drumlins, kettles, and moraines. More than any other state, Wisconsin wears its geology on its face. Incredibly slow-moving rivers of ice flowed down through what is now Canada. The glaciers carved and scoured. They picked up boulders and dropped them hundreds of miles later.

Over thousands of years the glaciers advanced, then retreated. The last Ice Age ended around 12,000 years ago. Like giant fingers, the lobes of the glaciers put their imprint on the state. The actions of the glaciers explain why Wisconsin's landscape varies so dramatically. Within a mile you can descend from the top of a wooded hill to a grassy prairie and then wander into swampy wetlands.

As the land was carved, the resulting low-lying areas formed into thousands of small and not-so-small lakes. Each variation in the land resulted in different wildlife, plants, trees and even fungi, all adapted to their specific habitat.

More than sixty years ago, Ray Zillmer had a

vision: to create a national park that traced the edges of those "fingers" or lobes of glaciers when they retreated from Wisconsin at the end of the last Ice Age. He wanted to protect the unique geological features that were left behind.

Zillmer passed his vision to Representative Henry Reuss, who helped to create the Ice Age National Scientific Reserve, giving special status to nine sites across Wisconsin. These natural treasures were to be connected by a foot path. And thus, Wisconsin's Ice Age Trail was born.

As part of the National Park System, the trail is built and maintained by the Ice Age Trail Alliance. Individual chapters are coordinated in the counties through which the trail passes, piecing together a patchwork of private landowners, county, state, and federally owned lands. Volunteers continue to build and maintain the trail. Until the trail is completed, unofficial road connectors link the separate segments.

Your two authors, Sylvia Oberle and Kris Rued-Clark, fell in love with the trail many years ago. Sylvia completed all 1,093 miles of the trail in 2011. As of this writing, Kris has completed about one-third of the trail, with intentions to walk the entire trail, section by section.

Some people who walk the trail are through-hikers, doing it all at once. The majority are section hikers, completing a section at a time, in no particular order. Most begin close to home, get hooked on the trail, and commit to finishing it. About 40 percent of Wisconsinites live within 30 minutes of the trail.

For this book we have put together what we consider the "greatest hits" of the Ice Age Trail that would be appropriate for many age levels. We suggest you plan a vacation around the trail and allow time to explore nearby locales. Many places the trail passes through were parks before the trail was built, due to the natural beauty of the

nearby lakes, rivers, or streams.

The trail varies greatly, from moderately difficult to flat and smooth. In several segments, old railroad beds have been converted to trail, and walkers share the path with bicyclists. These sections are ideal for strollers and wheelchairs.

Our favorite places to walk are in the woods and by the water, but we also love walking through small towns and larger cities. You come to know a place so much more intimately when you have traversed it on foot.

Come discover some of our favorites parts of the trail with us, and bring along your children, your friends' children, your nieces and nephews, your grandchildren. Let them discover this amazing place that we call home. See how the glaciers have carved our state into the many-faceted gem that it is.

Before you walk:

We have written this book so that you can find and explore these highlighted sections with no further assistance. However, to make the most of your adventure, it's best that you refer to the official trail guides of the Ice Age Trail Alliance: the Ice Age Trail Atlas, and the Ice Age Trail Companion Guide. We also suggest that you call chapter coordinators to check current conditions, go to the Ice Age Trail website, and pay attention to the weather. One of our most memorable adventures involved wading through thigh-high water across a creek that is normally a "rock hop." Three days of rain prior to our walk had swollen the streams.

A few words about safety:

The Ice Age Trail is an all-season experience. You don't need fancy clothes or expensive equipment. Just dress accordingly. Sturdy, comfortable shoes are essential. In wet areas, boots or waterproof shoes are a blessing. Plan ahead, dress in layers, and pay careful attention to the yellow blazes marking the trail.

Small packs or clothes with multiple pockets are handy for snacks, sandwiches, and lots of water. Bring insect repellent and sunscreen or wear a hat. For added safety, take along a compass or GPS and flashlight. Cellphones can be handy, especially if you're shuttling, and we both consider our cameras to be essential trail gear. Most important, bring a sense of adventure. Allow time to sit on a fallen log or dangle your bare feet from a wooden bridge into the cooling waters of a stream.

As Dianne Genz, another 1,000-miler, says, "The trail gets to you. Once you start, it keeps calling you back."

Tenderfoot Hiker
Superior Lobe

"A fifty-mile hike? Why would you want to do that?" That was the question Gene, my husband, asked as I waved the newspaper article in front of his nose that morning.

It took awhile to make him understand that I thought it would be great to get outdoors for a long hike. Hiking on the Ice Age Trail, taking photos, learning to identify rocks and plants appealed to me. It didn't matter if the rest of the family thought I was a little crazy.

I had no tips on proper gear, but I was about to learn. In my duffle, I just threw some jeans, a jacket and my comfortable Nikes. I packed some disposable plastic boots used by barn inspectors just in case of rain.

Fresh air and September weather greeted the group as we assembled for the first day of our trek, sponsored by the Superior Lobe Chapter of the Ice Age Trail. We started near Brill, Wisconsin, in Barron County. It was neat to see trees with a few red leaves shining in the sun, but I was most impressed by the trees the beavers had cut down. Near the beaver dam I saw several fallen trees, some hewn to the center that looked like the work of some powerful sawing machine. Beaver teeth! I took photos proving "working like a beaver" is not just an idle saying.

Closer to the ground I saw bottle gentian, a new plant to me. Wild black-eyed Susan grew beside the trail and seemed to look up at us with their brown button eyes in a circle of yellow petals. We saw soft, fuzzy cattails near the water as we hiked along the wetland. Later, I snapped a picture of the abandoned heron rookery. I counted 55 huge nests. So many good sights to see!

The next day it started to mist, then turning into real rain. So I donned my clear plastic boots. Proudly hiking in my comfortable Nikes, I thought I was pretty cool. My boots surprised and amused fellow hikers who teased and called me "The Barn Boot Girl." And the boots worked fine. For a while, that is.

Rain pattered down steadily the next day while we did some interesting road walk. Some Barron County streets have names that end in ½ and ¼.

I was told people here love this type of street marking because they know exactly how many miles to the next corner. It's good to know how different counties do things.

The rain kept pouring down. No bother to me, until we came to the Tuscobia Trail. At first, I took some pictures of beautiful birches over a small kettle lake with a hint of fall showing on the red sumac leaves. The next part gave me trouble. Here we trod on sharp gravel because the trail followed an abandoned rail line. A special kind of quartzite rocks had been imported there many years ago. These chunky rocks cut right through my thin plastic boots. My boots were being shredded at every step. I walked along for miles with wet feet.

I didn't think wet feet would matter, and soon the trail went back into the forest. As I walked up

and down hills, my wet toes were pushing to the front of my shoes. It didn't take long to get sore toes hiking down hills. Up and down we went. Some hills were pretty steep, and what goes up must come down. On the way down, I had to put on my brakes. On every downhill, my toes hurt more and more as they pushed harder against my shoes. I only lasted another day and a half. Then, I called Gene to come and get me. My toes were hurting and felt like they were on fire. But what do neophytes know? Live and learn.

One of the hikers had told me about a wonderful tape called moleskin. I bought some. After two days at home, I found out how far my friends were and was able to join them on the last day of the hike. When they saw me a cheer went up for Barn Boot Girl! And with moleskin toes so nice and cozy, I hiked those last miles to the finish line. What a great feeling!

We watched and cheered the young man who had done the most Ice Age Trail miles to date. He was presented with a walking staff and proclaimed a star hiker. I began to wonder, "Might I do that?" I looked around and saw my new friend, Laura the expert birder, who had informed me about heron habitat. Next to her, I saw the smiling woman who told me she was planning her next hike on the Appalachian Trail.

We gathered around the trail marker smiling and posing for a group picture to be displayed at a restaurant called Adventures. All that enthusiasm was catching. That night I went home and said to my family, "I'm going to hike the whole one thousand miles of the Ice Age Trail!"

– Sylvia

St. Croix Falls Segment
(including Gandy Dancer Segment)
Polk County

The western terminus of the Ice Age Trail, the St. Croix Falls segment, features volcanic basalt bedrock and contains unique potholes, some large enough to hold a person (16 feet deep and 3 feet wide). Glacial melt water wore down the rock and silt in a drilling motion making the pothole and rock forms. The rocky cliffs have walkout sections where hikers can look out over the St. Croix River. Rock climbers can sometimes be seen here practicing their sport. Pothole Trail is a short loop but a bit rugged. Follow signs and step safely.

A more difficult section, but very scenic, is hiking along the scenic shoreline and crossing the log path and a ford at Big Rock Creek that has no bridge. The ups and downs of this section add to the adventure.

The Ice Age Trail shares the Gandy Dancer Bike trail in Polk County. It follows an abandoned railroad bed and is named after the railroad workers using Gandy Company tools. Working and singing in harmony they were called "Gandy Dancers."

This is a flat and easy walk with the path flanked by a variety of trees.

This section is part of the Superior Lobe of the Wisconsin Glacier which covered the region more than 10,000 years ago. A lobe is a tongue –shaped terrain made when the glacier receded. Wisconsin has five lobes. The Superior Lobe is on the western border of our state.

The trail is on an outwash plain and runs along some of Polk County's best farmland.

Hiking north it passes Milltown and goes on to the city of Luck. Both towns have interesting places to visit. A new library featuring Native Americans and first settlers has been built in Luck. This library is an excellent place to browse and spend time.

Options:

¼ mile loop: St. Croix Interstate Park Pothole Trail

3.5 miles: From Lion's Park (just off Highway 87, three miles north of St. Croix Falls) to Interstate Park

4 miles: On Gandy Dancer IAT part of trail, hike from Milltown to Luck

6.5 miles: Hike north on the Gandy Dancer Trail from Centuria to Milltown

Smile and "Bear" It

Time can seem to stand still on a nice sunny day in the summer. It did for me, as I hiked the Gandy Dancer Trail near Milltown, Wisconsin. I had just started my tenth mile, when out of the bushes stepped a big black bear! We both froze and it was a "stare eye" contest. With barely six feet between us, I was awed by the sight of this tall bear and kept thinking, "Is this for real?" Neither of us knew what to do. Time stood still.

I smiled to myself and thought, "You knew this could happen. Now, what are you going to do about it?" It's amazing how many thoughts can run through your mind in a second. I leaned forward a bit hoping the bear would run, but he just stood there looking. Without turning, I took two steps back and noticed some raspberries. The raspberries made me think of the time Uncle Bill was picking berries and thought a neighbor was picking on the opposite side of the patch. He was very surprised when he saw the black bear. Bill picked slowly and steadily away, unnoticed. "If it worked for Uncle, it will work for me," I thought. So I picked a berry and ate it right in front of that bear! The bear did what seemed like a few dance steps with soft ballet feet, turned to the west, and ambled off into the bushes.

It was an adventure to see the bear, and I do think most people in Northern Wisconsin do well living with this form of wildlife. The DNR tells us there are 13,000 (and probably more) black bear in Wisconsin. The bear are very healthy at the present time. It has been reported they are having three or four cubs more often. Also, bear density has been expanding southward in Wisconsin.

All we need to do is adjust to a few sensible rules. Don't feed the bear. It's against the law. Food put out, or garbage left about will keep the bear coming back and make them dependent and out of their habitat.

A friend told me about a bumping noise he heard one night. He looked out the window and saw nothing but black. "Where's the moon?" he thought. He soon found a black bear, back pressed against the window, shaking the bird feeder to get the seeds!

The bear may make visits to the corn fields in the fall. One year, we had seven bear in our town. We had one mother and two cubs in a tree at a residence and another in the park with her three cubs. The police just took a yellow ribbon and roped off the area. They said the bear would soon go quietly back to their own area. And they did.

Photos by Rick Koziel

When you are camping, put your food in a bear box. Do not keep food in your tent. While camping with a group, we were not allowed to keep even toothpaste in our tent. An ounce of prevention makes sense. Extra precaution may include bringing in grills, bird feeders and pet food at night.

The black bear is an interesting and beneficial animal in Wisconsin, as well as a thrilling subject to observe, photograph, and to study. Of course, these activities must be carried out safely with respect for both bear and people. I am putting my bear sighting on my list of high adventure. You can, too. When you see a big black bear, for a few moments, time may just stand still.

– Sylvia

Hikes for Tree Lovers and Tree Huggers

The clearest way to the universe is through forest wilderness.
– John Muir

Hiking the trail to enjoy the variety and beauty of Wisconsin trees is fun in any season. We see the spring green of April and May, the deep green foliage and shade of summer, the snow-laden boughs of winter, and especially the beautiful fall colors.

Fall is the time when nights grow longer, and chlorophyll slows down, allowing the red and yellow of the leaves to shine in the sun. Sunlight and a bright, blue sky also can enhance, making colorful leaves even brighter. It's an ideal time to show the children the various species or just give them an appreciation of the trees in our lives. The trail's high plateaus, bluffs, and towers give breathtaking views as we look out over an expanse of fall color.

Options for short hikes:

3.2 miles: Polk County, Straight River Segment
Parking near Highway 48 (Ice Age Trail Atlas Map 4f-3f)

2.5 miles: Taylor County, Wood Lake Segment
Parking at trailhead on Tower Road (Ice Age Trail shares blue blaze markers around lake)

1.8 miles: Chippewa County, Chippewa River Segment
County Road Z to County Road CC (Ice Age Trail Atlas Map 16f)

1.6 mile loop: Dane County, Lodi Segment
On Riddle Road go 2 miles south to trailhead.
Parking on Springfield Road (Ice Age Trail Atlas Map 63f)

3.1 miles: Langlade County, Highland Lake Eastern Segment
Highway 45 to Forest Road (Ice Age Trail Atlas Map 33f)

Marathon County, Eau Claire Dells Segment
   1 mile: Parking in County Park (Ice Age Trail Map 40f)

    2 miles: Marathon County Road Z to Sportsman Drive (Ice Age Trail Atlas Map 40f)

2 miles: Marquette County, John Muir Memorial Park Segment (Ice Age Trail Atlas Map 56f)

Woodland Wonder

After the glaciers melted the land warmed and forests grew. Our first explorers wrote in their journals about the grand sight of great oaks, pines and other species found here in Wisconsin. The virgin timber is gone, but the many species live on as the forest continues to replenish itself. Enjoying the beautiful trees on the Ice Age Trail will please the single hiker or the entire family.

In Polk County, near Round Lake Road, I saw remarkable pines. There are signs on the trail for a short side-trip that directs you to a huge white pine. Sandy, a friend who sometimes hikes with me, wanted to see if we could reach around it. We joined our hands, and stretched our arms as far as we could around the tree. Our big "tree hug" went only a little over halfway around! The fragrance of the wood, pine needles and cones added pleasure to our walk. We took some pictures and decided our hike among the pines was a very good day.

Earlier in the year, I hiked along a curving esker

in Taylor County near Mondeaux Flowage and saw the yellow birches standing high on roots like octopus tendrils. It took a bit more time walking over those tree legs, but who minds when the scenery is good and the air is fresh? Yellow birch seedlings often start their growth inside rotted pine stumps. Here I was able to get a neat photo that looks almost like a painting.

On the Chippewa Lobe I had the pleasure of viewing some of the tallest aspen in Wisconsin. They grow on each side of the trail. You look up till your neck creaks, and it's hard to get a full photo in the viewer of your camera. I did get an especially good shot of a tall aspen with its gray trunk and green leaves against the blue October sky.

Near Lodi in Dane County stand gnarly oaks that are some of the oldest and largest bur oaks in Wisconsin. I hiked there in the fall with two grandsons and an exchange student from India. The student thought the view was breathtaking. He told us there are no oaks or maples where he lives in India. He marveled at the good trail, the open space and the colorful trees. Dane County also has many historic oaks on the Koltes Drumlin off Bong Road. And I have learned there is an Indian trail marker tree off Harbor Road near Westport. Kris, who often walks with me, is always looking for those marker trees. We will be sure to visit that tree on a future hike in Dane County.

On hikes in Langlade County one can see the scenic tamarack trees that grow around kettle lakes made by the glacier. In fall, their golden reflections in the water make photos worthy of any postcard. They are the only conifers that shed

their needles in autumn. I've heard of people who didn't know that fact and cut their tamarack trees down by mistake, thinking their trees were dead. If only they had known more about trees!

Near Hatley in Marathon County, I photographed perfectly shaped elms. Their dark umbrella shapes look majestic against the winter snow at twilight. In Marquette County, one can take a side trip and visit the forested hill where John Muir spent many hours of his boyhood.

In Barron County I saw large poplar trees that beaver also love and use to build massive lodges and dams. It's a wonder to look at these trees and know a beaver can cut down such a big tree.

Near Fawn Avenue in Taylor County, I learned how to identify the hemlock tree thanks to the little signs along the trail naming some of the prominent species. The Chequamegon National Forest has wonderful trees and a great variety. I vow to learn more about Wisconsin trees and plant at least one. I encourage all those who like the forest to choose a section of the Ice Age trail and take a walk. As you learn Wisconsin glacial geology, you'll be sure to take note of the many great trees.

In the words of Zona Gale:

Trees have intelligence and spirit is combined with them to some degree.

– Sylvia

Ode to Autumn Trees

Oak and hardwood trees so fine
Needles long, pitch of pine

Seed of cottonwood, twine of vine
Yellow birches, stately pine

Leaf of basswood round and spacious
Trunk of elm so tall and gracious

Heartwood, sapwood, cork do vary
Tasty fruit, walnut, apple, cherry

Sylvan wood divine
Forest treasure mine.

– Sylvia

Pine Lake and Straight River Segments
Polk County

This segment has many scenic points. If you start at the Trade River Ski Trail parking lot and cross prairie open field to 140th road, the huge rocks at the start of this hike are impressive. You will see many unique triangular and round shaped boulders that are moss covered in the summer and stand like protective sentinels in fall and winter. The terrain is quite hilly at first then descending down to wetlands and prairie.

A tunnel channel was made by a fast-moving stream flowing out beneath the glacier as it was melting. Here the glacier carves a valley, its prominent feature. The Straight River tunnel channel

is one of the best examples of this glacial feature in Wisconsin. Good for walking and very scenic.

The trail follows an esker, a ridge of sand and gravel deposited by the glacier by streams that flowed at its base. Hiking on top of the esker is easy and fun. The Polk County Ice Age Trail has some of the best eskers in Wisconsin.

Straight Lake Wilderness State Park is a new state park featuring wildlife area, mature hardwood forests, and three flowages. Habitat for plants and bird species is plentiful and one may see ruffed grouse fly up or an eagle soaring above.

Options:

2 miles: To recreate the Blue Moon Hike, take Highway 48 and go 8.5 miles east of Luck. Stay on 260th Avenue when Highway 48 veers off, and continue one-half mile to 70th Street. Go north one-half mile to the parking lot on the left. Follow the trail as it loops.

3 miles: Parking on 280th Avenue to parking on 100th Street (County Road I)

6 miles: Begin at Trade River Ski Trail parking lot, 4.5 miles north of Luck off Highways 35/48 to parking on Highway 48, 5.5 miles east of Luck at 9th Street

Once in a Blue Moon

Think about what you might do "once in a blue moon." Would you do a bungee jump, sky dive, or go on an exotic vacation? Not me. I went for a hike.

The Ice Age Trail Superior Lobe Indianhead Chapter had a "Blue Moon" hike August 31, 2012. It was held on the Pine Lake segment and covered about two miles of forest and prairie. About thirty hikers started from the Ice Age Trail parking lot near Highway 48.

What a neat evening! We watched the moon as it peeked through the trees on a late summer night. Everyone stepped up the pace a little in the forest part because we wanted to get to open prairie for a better view. Two miles was just about the right distance for the small children and they loved it! A telescope was set up so everyone could view a close-up of the August 31st blue moon. Lots of Oh's and Ah's filled the cool night air.

The moon has been a part of my life from the time I was little. Sitting in the backseat traveling at night with my parents, I marveled at how the moon seemed to follow us. It made me feel important and secure. In my mind, the moon was watching over us. My favorites were the orange harvest moons with their big round faces. New moons, first quarter moons, and last quarter moons shaped like bananas, I loved them all.

Children have a special fascination when it comes to the moon. Grandson Charles, at age two, would look out the big window and say "Moon, Moon." It was probably one of his first ten words. This fascination is proven by the popular children's book Good Night Moon by Margaret Wise Brown and illustrated by Clement Hurd. First published in 1947, by 1953 it had sold 1,500 copies. By 1990, the book had sold four million. Today, if you go to YouTube you can see the colorful pages turned as the poem is sung to you while the moon shines through the window.

Just what is a blue moon? The space channel tells me it's not really blue. There can be a hint

of blue in any full moon. It's possible the moon looked blue to our ancestors when they were looking through forest fire smoke or volcanic dust. Nowadays, we call the second full moon in a month a blue moon. This only occurs about every 2.5 years. That's how the term came to mean something that doesn't happen very often.

After becoming a "Thousand Miler" I can't believe I'm back on the Ice Age Trail.

I thought I'd hike the IAT only "once in a blue moon." I have decided to do the new sections. So far, I have done the Gibraltar Rock segment near Lodi in Columbia County and the new section along the Poplar River in Marathon County. Maps are available on Ice Age Trail.com.

My advice to you: Don't wait for "once in a blue moon" to walk. Many chapters sponsor full moon hikes and snowshoe hikes as well. Let's see you out there on the trail or on your favorite walk in the moonlight.

– Sylvia

Superior Lobe
Hemlock Creek & Tuscobia Trail Segments
Barron and Washburn Counties

You will see a variety of scenery when hiking the Ice Age Trail in Rusk, Barron, and Washburn Counties. Hills, outwash plain, sedge meadow and a trail that follows an old railroad bed will make your hike interesting and fun. On hazy days looking east you may see the Blue Hills, consisting of erosion-resistant red quartzite topped with a thin layer of glacial deposits.

The Hemlock Creek Segment has a 2.7 mile loop that makes a good scenic hike. It may be just right, if you are hiking with family and friends and want to enjoy a morning or an afternoon in the fresh air. The spring-green of the trees in early June, new foliage around the wooden bridge, and the bubbling creek gives you a feeling of freshness and renewal. This creek was used for logging in

the past. You can still see remnants of that history.

On the trail near the wetlands and on kettle lakes you will see waterfowl: ducks, geese, herons, cranes and more. If you are lucky you may even see an occasional owl roosting on a limb in the daytime. Many species of wildlife build their homes in this part of Wisconsin. For example, if you hike in summer you may come upon a deer with twin fawns or many smaller animals like squirrels, chipmunks and rabbits. There are several beaver dams and you can see gnawed trees in the process of being cut down by the beaver.

The Great Wisconsin Birding and Nature Trail is a side trip that will interest birders. It is located a little over a mile south of the Finohorn Road Segment. Also, the Superior Lobe Chapter sponsors a fall color hike each year from the CASTA Cumberland ski area to Barronett. To view color at its peak, contact the Superior Lobe IAT web page for date and time.

Options:

2.7 mile loop around Hemlock Creek: From Birchwood, travel southwest on State Highway 48 to County Road F, turn right and go south 8 miles to Murphy Flowage Recreation Area

5.5 miles: Hike from County Road F to trailhead at Finohorn Road

4.7 miles: Hike 30th Avenue to town of Brill or Brill to 30th Avenue (Tuscobia Segment)

5 miles: Tuscobia Trail. From Rice Lake take Highway 48 northeast to County Road SS trailhead, which is 4.5 miles north of Rice Lake. Hike east from trailhead to town of Brill. (This hike is on an abandoned railroad bed. It crosses Tuscobia Creek and has an interesting spur trail with a glacial rock and Aldo Leopold bench.)

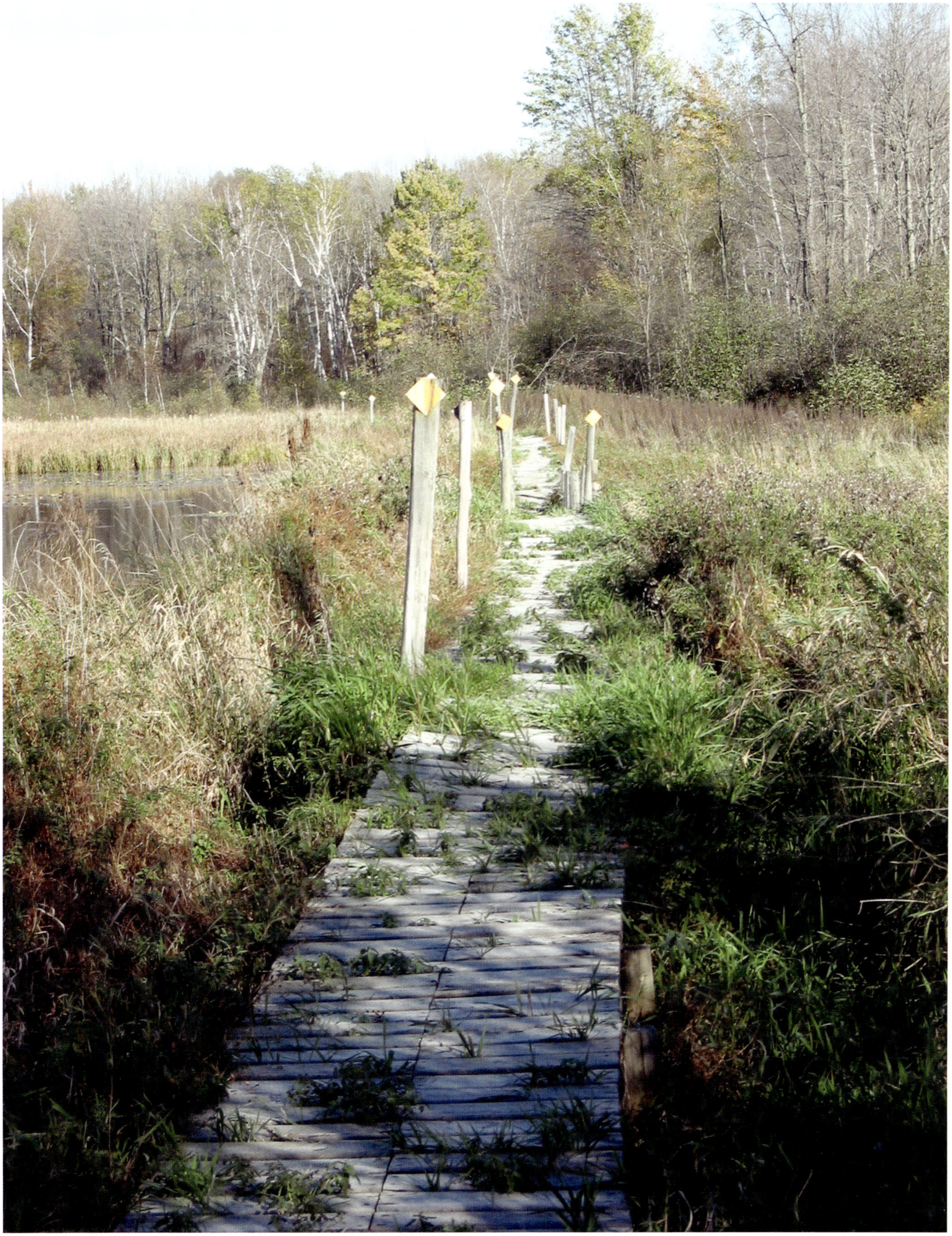

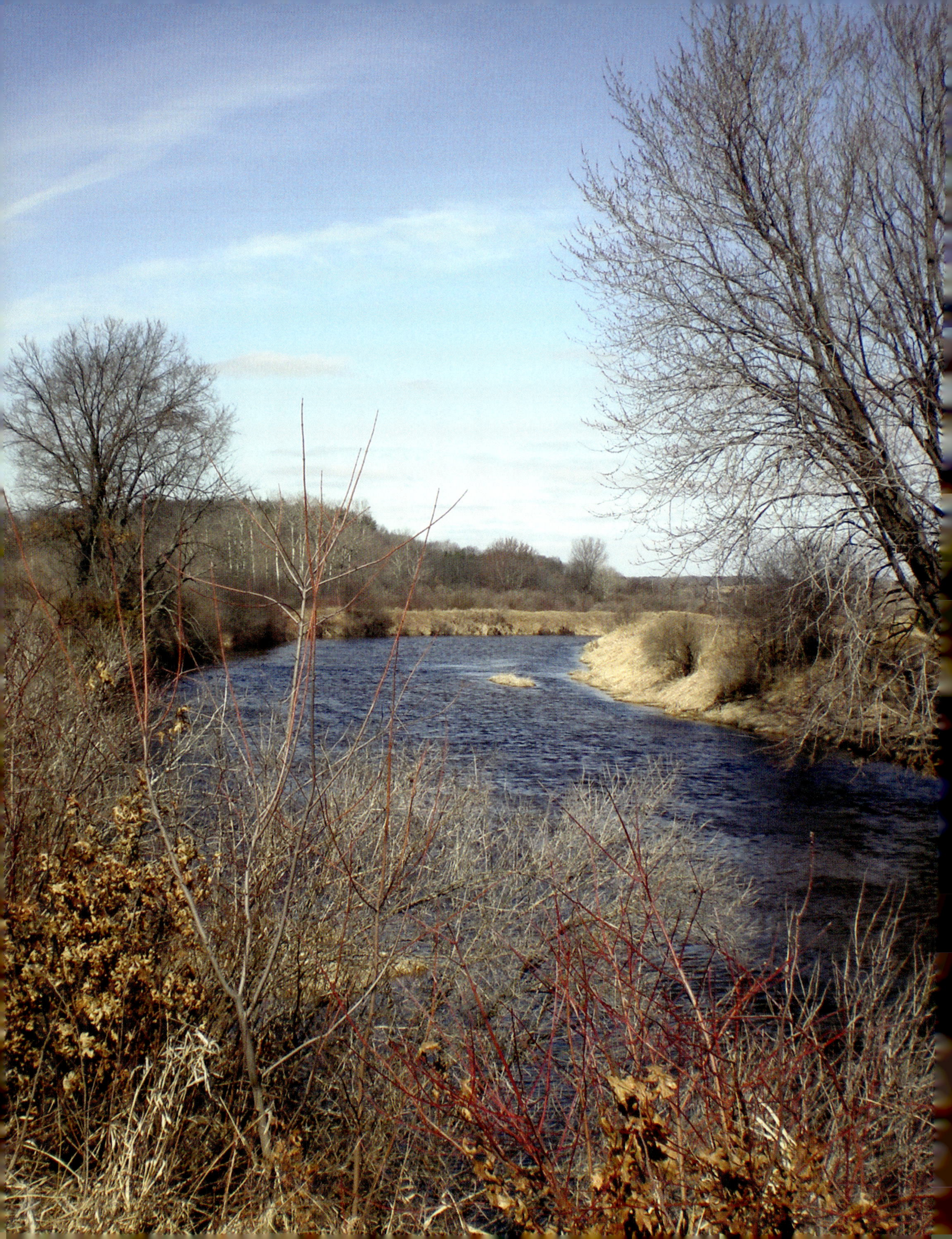

Chippewa Moraine Segment
Chippewa County

Ten thousand years ago when glacial ice melted, some of it formed huge chunks. Debris was deposited on the sides and top, burying the ice. When the ice melted, many kettle lakes were formed. On the Chippewa Moraine segment you will walk along these lakes amid gentle hills and forest cover of ash, oak and maple.

If you decide to take a late summer hike in August you will find ripe blackberries hanging on the bushes. Wild asters, light blue and white border the trail. Frogs and turtles are abundant on and near the lakes. You may see squirrels, rabbits and an occasional black bear. This section is also home for a variety of birds: nuthatch, jays, wrens, cranes and more.

A visit to the center before and after the hike offers displays and hands-on exhibits. You can view some live snakes, turtles and frogs to touch and view. A fur display you can touch helps identify animals you might see on the trail. Boards showing glacial features light up the exhibit room. A naturalist or trail expert is on hand to teach and explain.

You might also want to purchase hats, pullovers, or T shirts.

A sunny day in summer is good. On fall day you can enjoy the color and swish in the leaves as you walk. A spring day with its budding trees and spring flowers is sure to please. A winter day trudging with your snow boots on is fine. A short snowshoe hike is fun, too. Any season, plan a hike with family or friends on the Chippewa Moraine.

Directions:
Chippewa Moraine Interpretive Center is 7 miles East of New Auburn on County Road M or 1.9 miles east of State Highway 40 on County Road M

Parking & maps available at the Interpretive Center

Options:
0.7 miles: Mammoth Nature trail

1.8 miles: Dry Lake Trail

4.5 mile loop: Circle Trail

6.5 miles: Interpretive Center to Plummer Lake Road

6.5 miles: Firth Lake Segment. County Road CC to County Road E

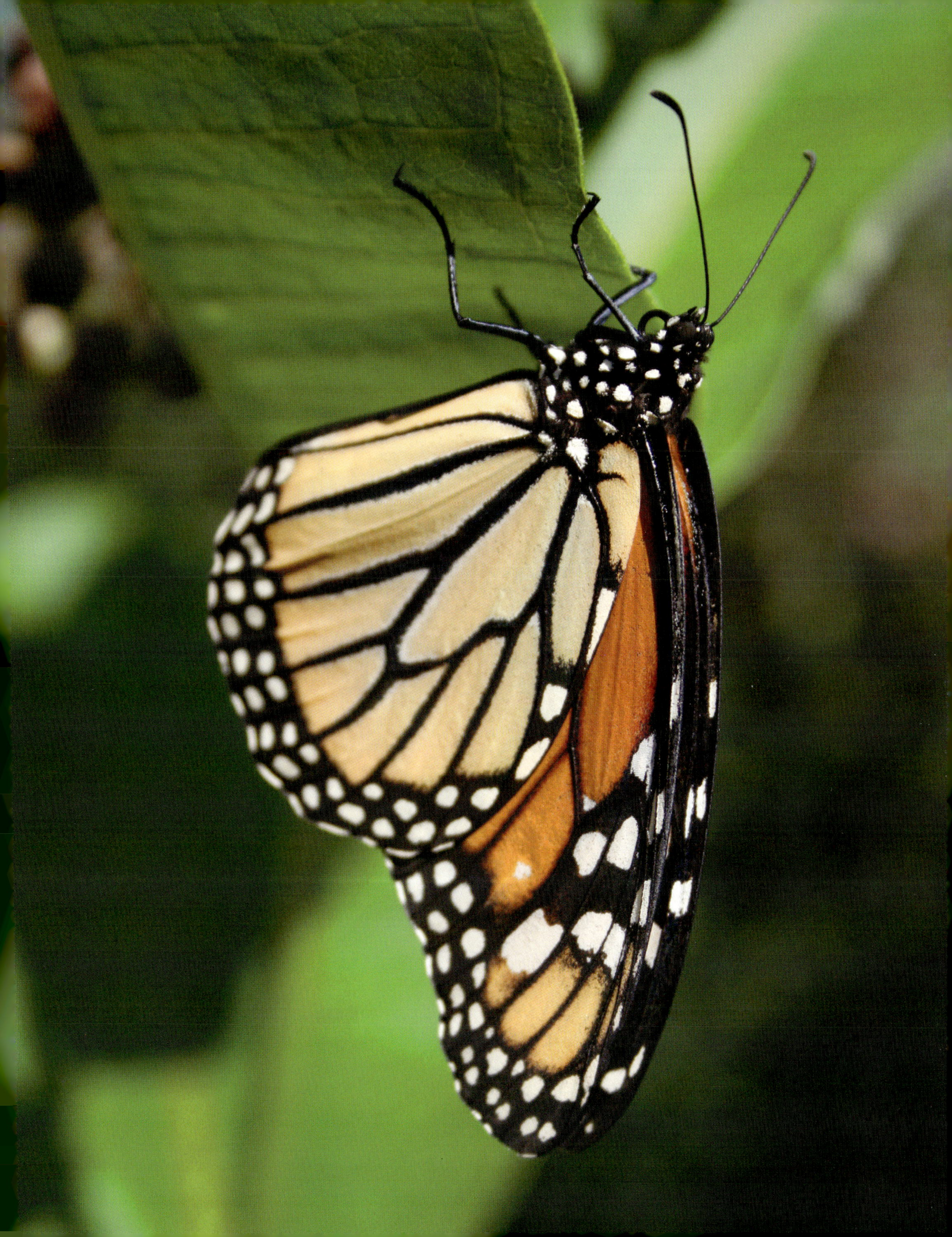

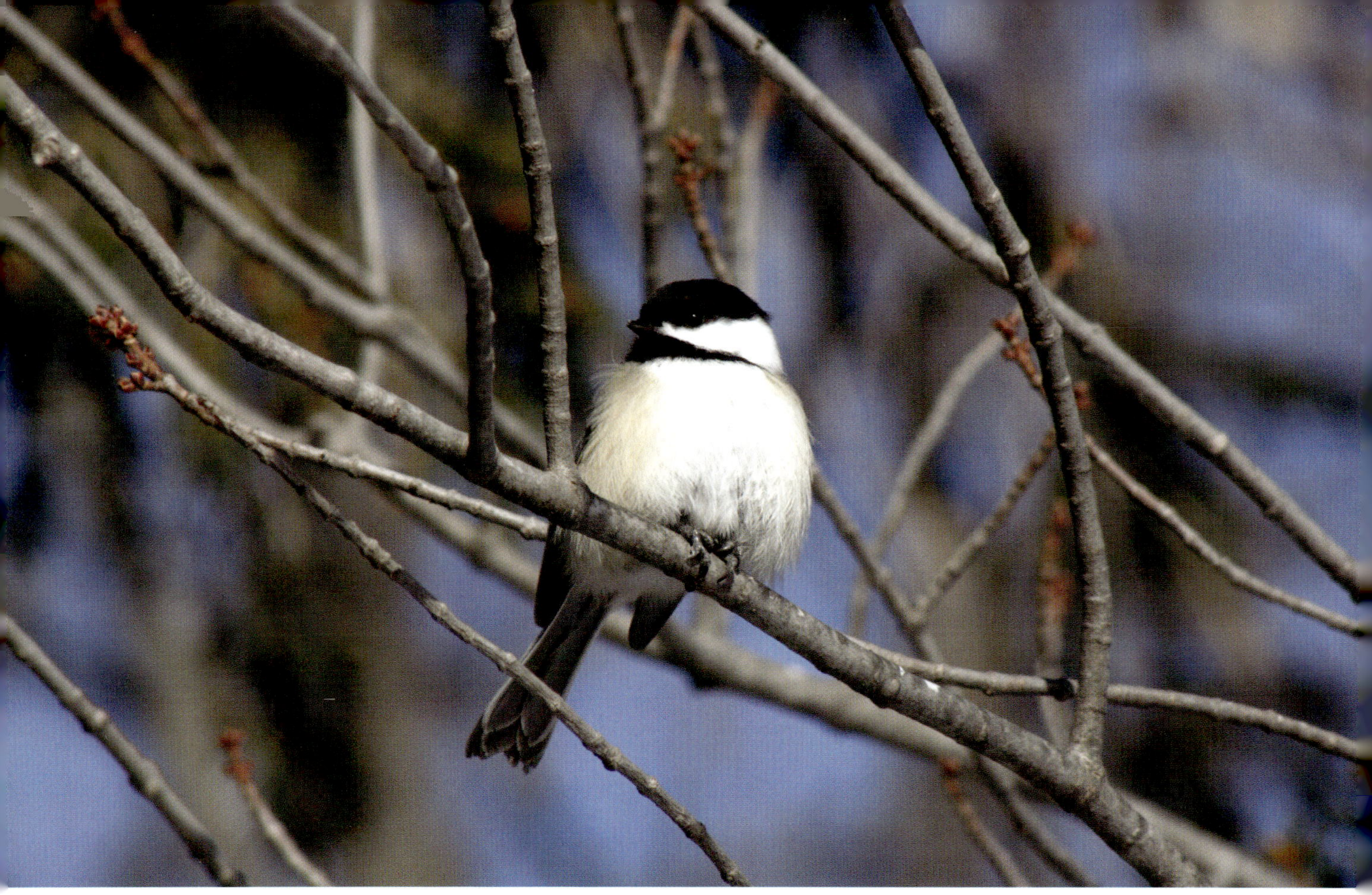
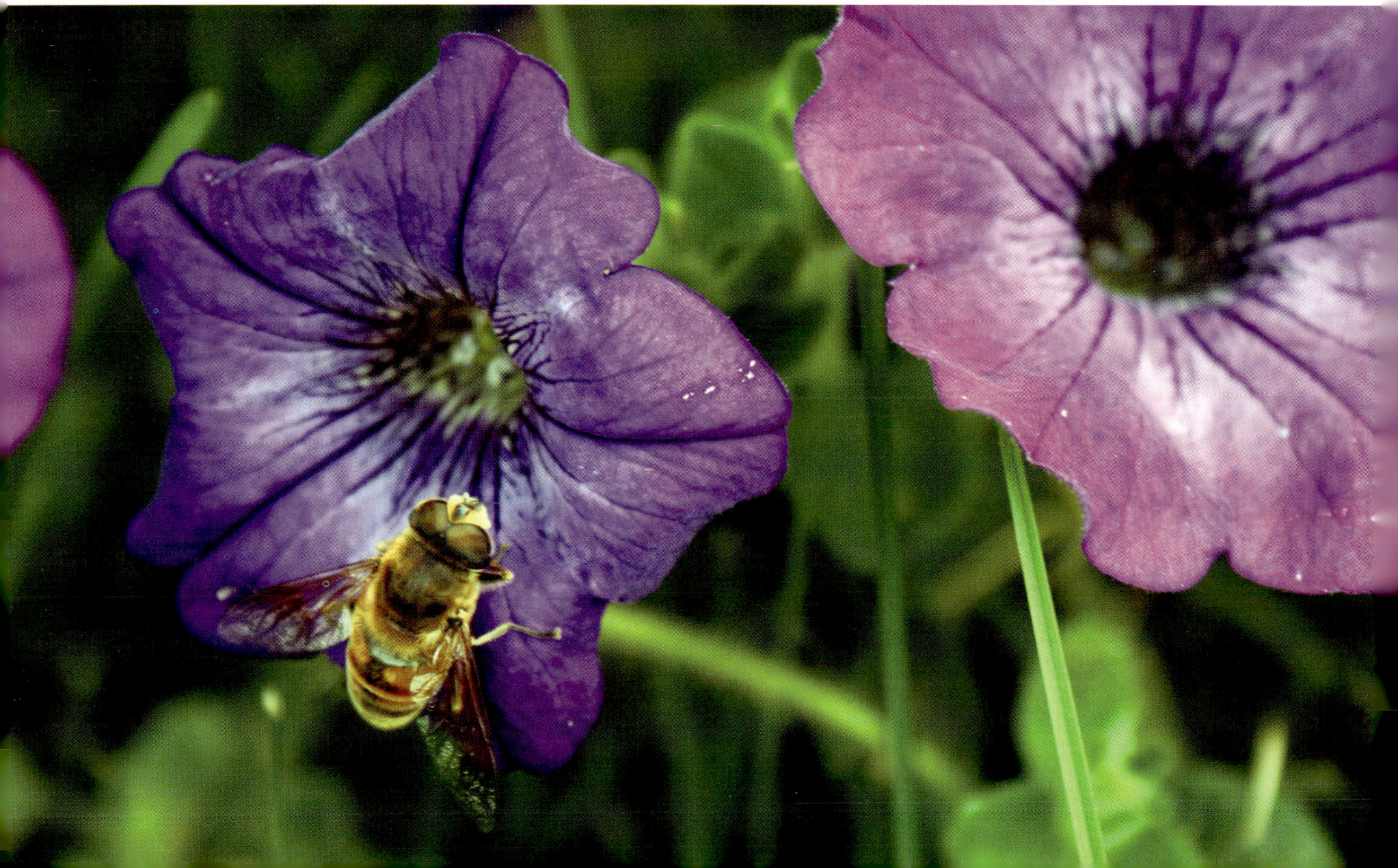

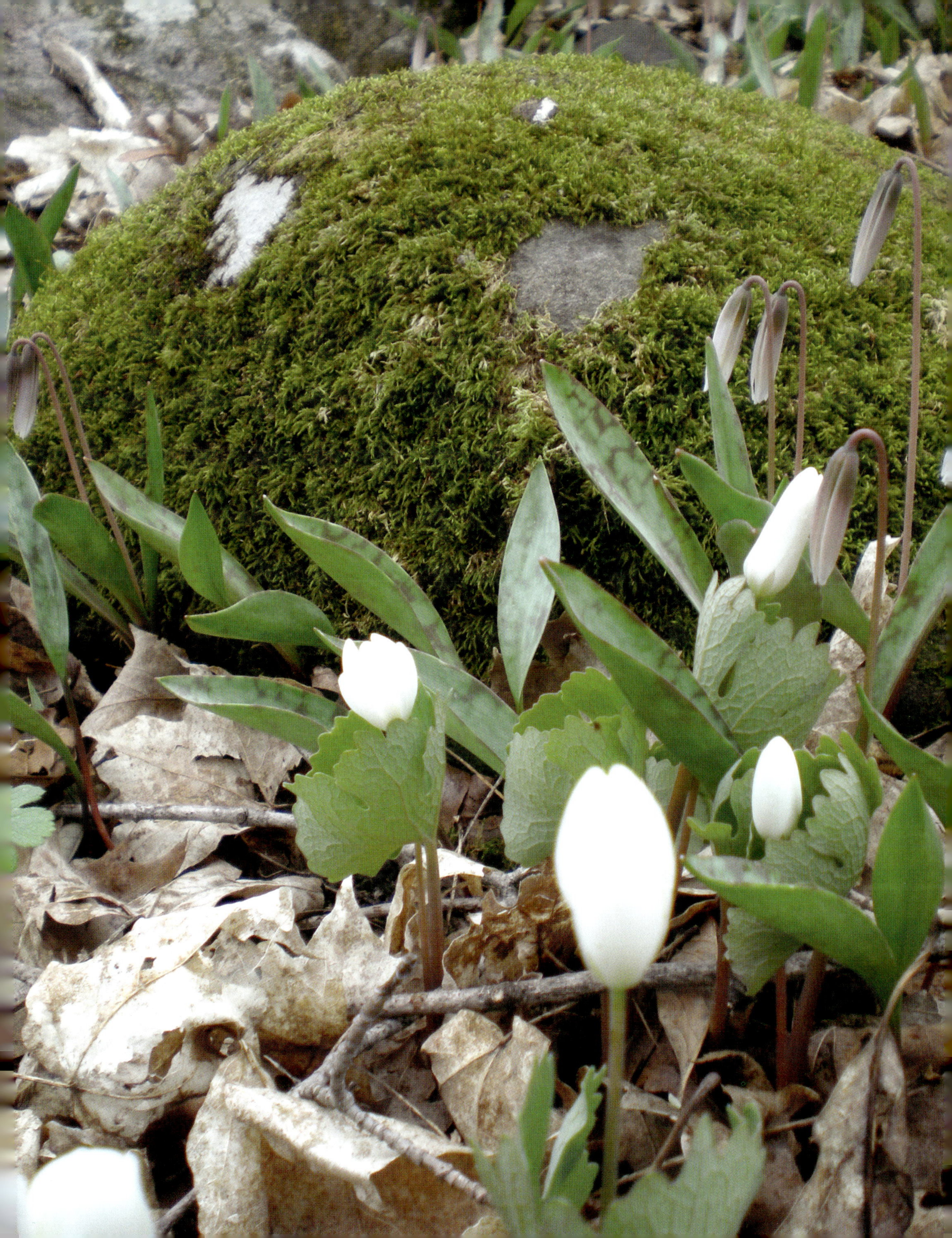

Ice Age Trail Adventure
Chippewa Moraine

"There's a turtle! Hurry! Get a picture." Gene hollered from the car. He made the three of us laugh so hard. Did he think I couldn't get my camera out in time to photograph a turtle? It was Gene's first time back as our driver since his heart attack due to a long-time bout with diabetes. He was out and about once more enjoying the summer weather and scenic views on our drive to the trail. And I'm sure he found the cheerful chatter of three women looking forward to a walk very pleasant.

Our plan was a five-mile hike starting at the Interpretive Center near New Auburn on the Chippewa Moraine. Everything was fresh and green on this beautiful 3rd of August. I took Gene's advice, hurried with my camera, and I did get the picture of the turtle as it slowly made its way to the side of the road. But the next photo op on the trail that day was a different story.

We started down the trail into the tall trees. Late summer weeds and wild asters bordered the trail. We had gone about a quarter of a mile when a black bear popped up out of the ferns and berry bushes! The bear froze and just looked. He was so clean with shiny black fur and a nice brown nose. In the excitement of the moment I fumbled with my camera, my fingers all thumbs. By the time I focused it, the bear turned. Kris was in the lead. She said, "Anyone have food?" I thought does she (this girl who talks to the animals-even snakes) want to entice the bear back for a picture? But I guess she was just being cautious. The bear looked back once more and slipped quietly back into the woods. We decided it was a junior bear abandoned by its mother, and that it was just bewildered being sent out on his own.

It was a thrill seeing the bear and it led to Caroline, Kris' sister from Germany, telling her story about the wild boar that city workers had to capture in her garden in Berlin. We walked along visiting and enjoying the fresh air. By late afternoon we finished the trek, and stopped in Bloomer for delicious kolaches and coffee.

– Sylvia

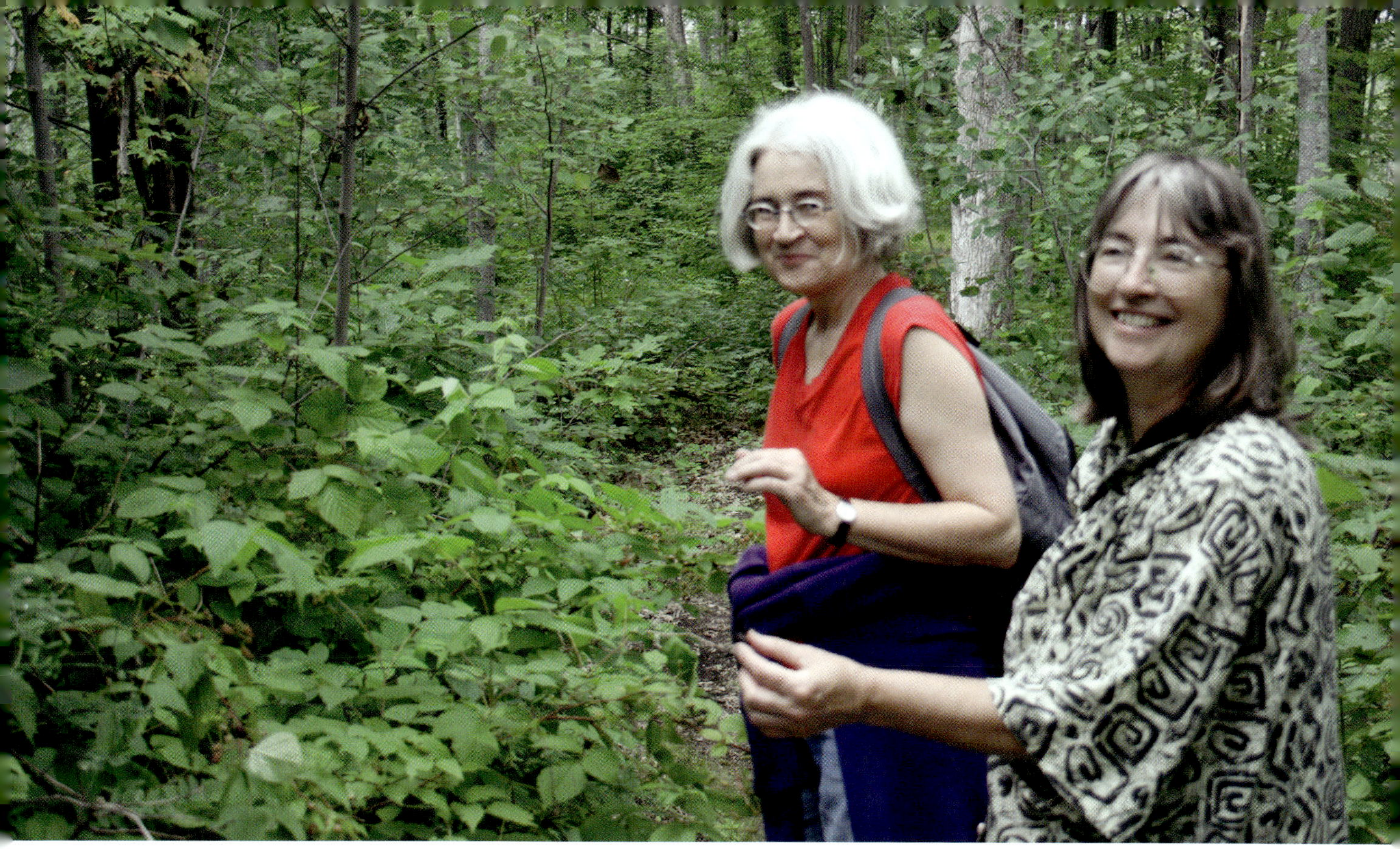

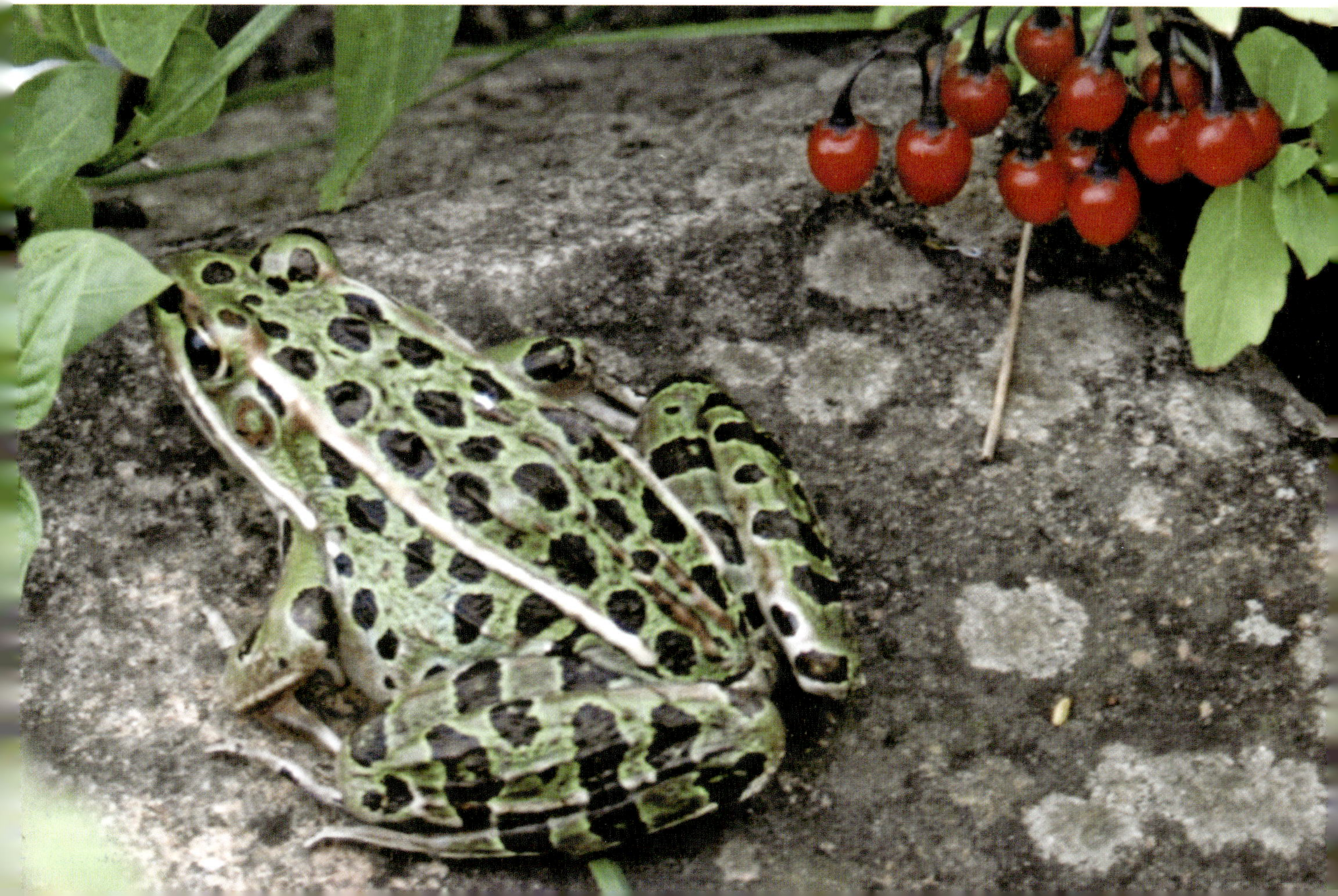

Mondeaux Esker Segment
Taylor County

The Mondeaux Esker Segment combines water, woods, and interesting geologic features such as eskers, which outline the western shore of the Mondeaux Flowage. On the western side, the trail climbs on the top of the Mondeaux Esker and follows the flowage for almost two miles before turning west into the woods.

This section of the trail traverses the Mondeaux Dam Recreation Area with campgrounds, swimming, and sheltered areas for picnics protected from the sun or rain. During the summer months, you may find a concession stand open at the historic lodge, which was built by the CCC.

If beginning your walk at the park area, you may choose to walk on either the east side or the west side of the water, returning to the park. A note of caution: the east side contains many rocks and tree roots crossing the trail. It can become tiring for younger hikers, so a shorter hike is advisable.

The Mondeaux Dam Recreation Area is an ideal setting for a picnic lunch or even camping. You may want to bring a canoe, kayak, or inflatable raft to enjoy paddling about in the placid waters. If visiting in the summer, bring along swimsuits, as the sandy beach area is rarely crowded.

Directions:

To reach Mondeaux Dam Recreation Area, from Westboro on State Highway 13, go west on County Road D for 6 miles. Turn left at Mondeaux Drive and go south for 1 mile. Turn right on Park Road and continue west to the recreation area.

Options:

Follow the Ice Age Trail on either the east side or the west side of Mondeaux Flowage, going almost two miles in either direction while still maintaining sight of the water and returning to the park area.

Mondeaux Esker

For Kris, the second section of the Ice Age Trail that she walked remains one of her favorites. In west-central Taylor county and part of the Chequamegon National Forest, the Mondeaux Esker segment follows both sides of the Mondeaux Florage and includes the Mondeaux Dam Recreation Area with campgrounds, swimming, boating, and a picnic area, plus toilets and water.

Being close to water makes even the hottest summer day feel a bit cooler, and in the fall, the brilliant oranges, reds and yellows of the leaves are reflected in the water. We walked this segment in late September when Wisconsin looks most glorious.

The trail continues past the recreation area through forest and meadows. We even saw signs of beavers in felled trees and the remaining stumps with the characteristic cone-shaped ends indicating beaver teeth had done the work.

Even though we enjoy walking on a weekday when most others are hard at work, this portion of the trail is never well traveled. Even when traveling with a family group, this part of the trail encourages quiet and contemplation.

Interpretive signs on the west side overlooking the water explain what an esker is and how kettle lakes were formed by the glacial ice. We also learned that the Mondeaux Flowage Area is on the Great Wisconsin Birding Nature Trail due to the abundance of birds to be seen.

– Kris

September Hike

Like children escaping
the stuffy classroom,
we bound out of the car,
begin our walk for the day.

The trail climbs a ridge that glaciers
carved out ten thousand years ago.
Too warm now, we tie our jackets
around our waists, rest a moment.

Below, the river curves
through forest, smoothes over rocks.
We hear the call of the cranes,
know they will fly south soon.

To be alive today, under this canopy
of blue and leaves so yellow and red,
it is enough.

– Kris

Photos by Kris Rued-Clark

Grandfather Falls Segment
Lincoln County

Following along the east bank of Wisconsin River, this segment of the trail makes for an interesting trip for several reasons: rapids, a dam and hydroelectric power plant, and huge wooden pipelines that carry water upriver from the reservoir created by the dam. Perhaps the most significant feature of this segment lies in its rock formations. Huge boulders line both sides of the river, and the rock formations that make up the river's bed are both visible and accessible from the trail.

The trail crosses a bridge by Grandfather Falls and follows the river for about a half-mile before coming out at a parking area by Grandfather Dam. Approximately two miles to the south is Camp New Wood County Park, which contains picnic areas, a toilet, and campground.

Fall is an excellent time to visit. If rainfall has been sparse, you may be able to climb onto the river's rocky and pot-holed bed, which would normally be covered in spring and times of high water.

If visiting this segment with young children, caution is advisable, yet there is something endlessly fascinating about watching the water cascading down next to the power plant. For an easy afternoon's adventure, park by Grandfather Falls, walk north to Grandfather Dam, and then walk back. If feeling ambitious, you could continue walking south to New Wood County Park. State Highway 107 follows close by. If younger children are ready to ride and the older children want to continue walking, you could easily accomplish this with one adult driving and another accompanying the walkers.

Directions:

From the intersection of I-39/Highway 51 and State Highway 64 in Merrill take State Highway 64 west for 3 miles. Turn right at State Highway 107 and go north 10 miles to New Wood County Park, or 11 miles to the Grandfather Falls parking area, or an additional 1.1 miles north to the trailhead and Hydro parking area.

September Journey
Wisconsin's Northwoods along the Wisconsin River

The day we walked the Grandfather Falls segment was one of those glorious fall days in Wisconsin. Bright blue sky, even brighter leaves, dressed in the reds, oranges, and yellows of autumn, and sunlight rippling on the water. We began our walk at New Wood County Park and ventured north on the trail.

We especially like walking on weekdays and imagining everyone else at work while we savor this season. If you choose to follow the branch of the trail to the east, you will venture through the Merrill School Forest and end up at Ripley Creek in about 1.5 miles. (There is no road access on this section, so you must turn around and go back the way you came in order to return to the park.)

We chose to go straight north, following the Wisconsin River. After about a mile we came to Grandfather Falls and the Hydro Plant. We stopped to take photos of the huge wooden tubes filled with water. These pipelines are used to carry water from the reservoir upriver. Remarkably, water spouted from numerous leaks, which we learned are repaired with wooden plugs. The tubes are constructed like barrels with wood and steel bands, as the wood will not corrode from the tremendous pressure of the water.

As we continued across the reservoir's floodgate outlet, the path took us into the woods and out on the riverbank. Here we took time to explore the rocks that have been worn into potholes and take even more pictures to remember our adventure by Grandfather Falls.

– Kris

October on the Ice Age Trail

(Kettlebowl Segment, Langlade County, October 12, 2008)

We shuffle-kick through leaf litter
green, orange, yellow, and brown
dew-dappled leaves.

Rising rich from forest floor,
damp perfume of leaves,
earth, and sweetgrass.

Startled, the ruffed grouse
rockets from nesting spot,
flashes through bare branches.

Over and over, old logging roads
cross, double back,
circle, converge, cross again.

In silence we walk, longing to hear
forgotten drumbeats,
calling, calling, calling.

– Kris

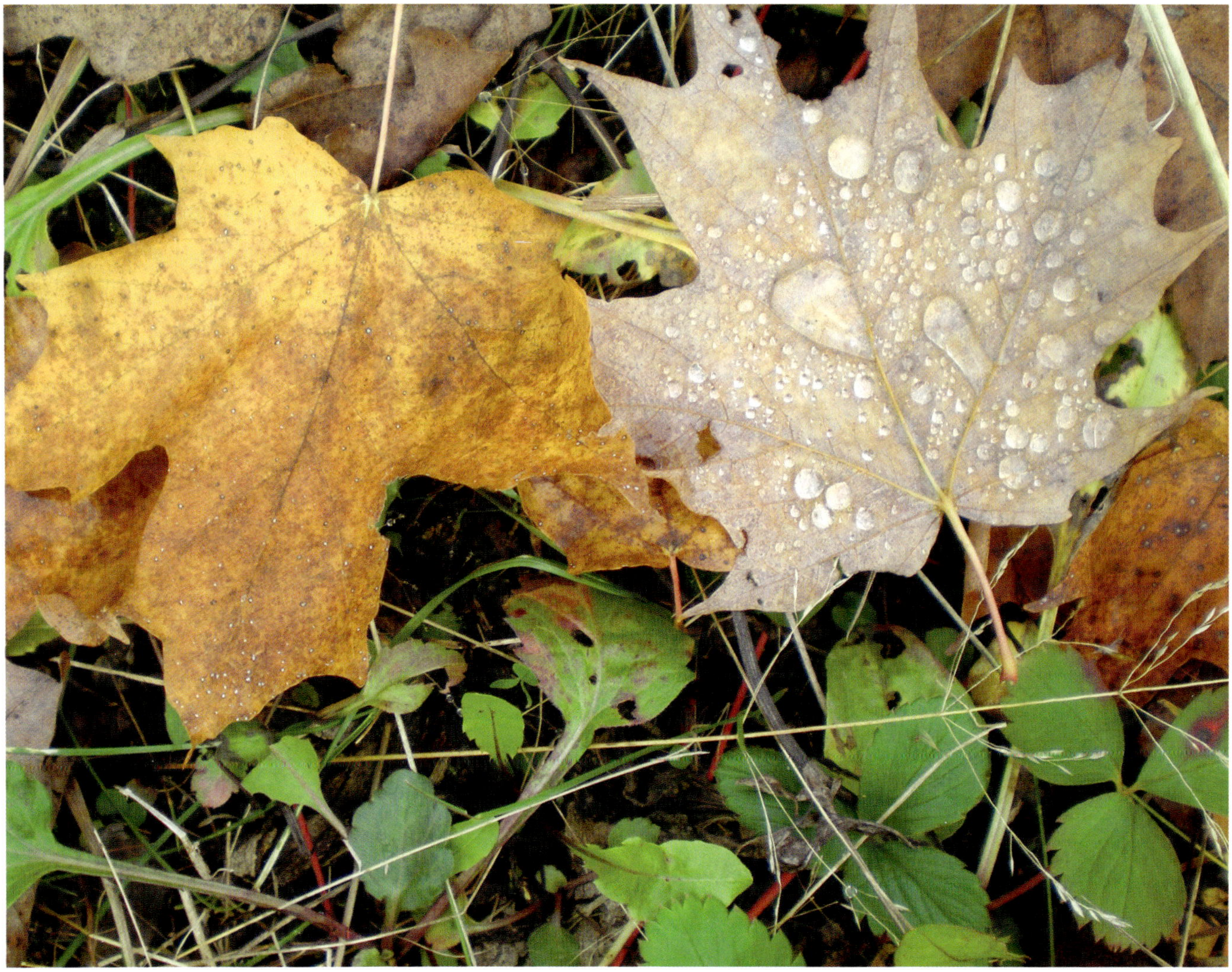

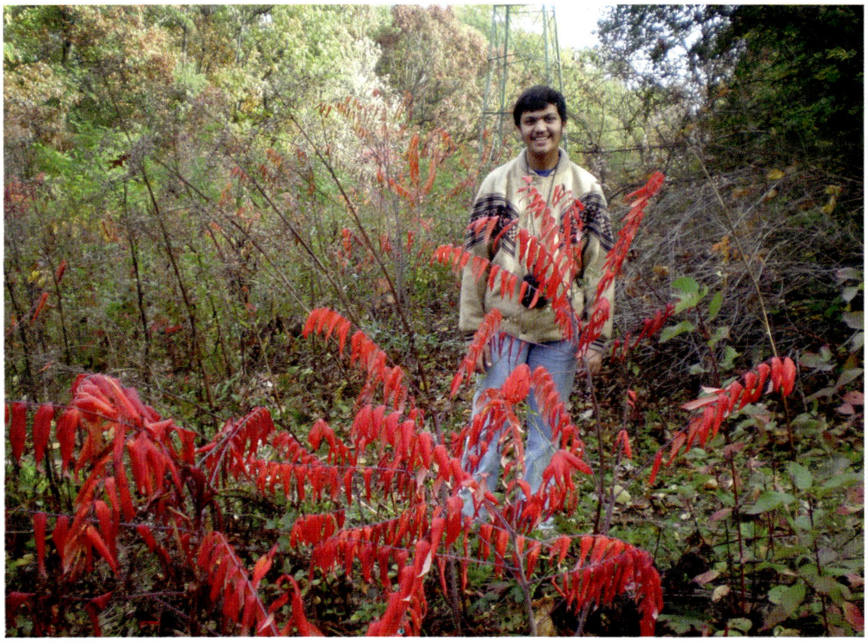

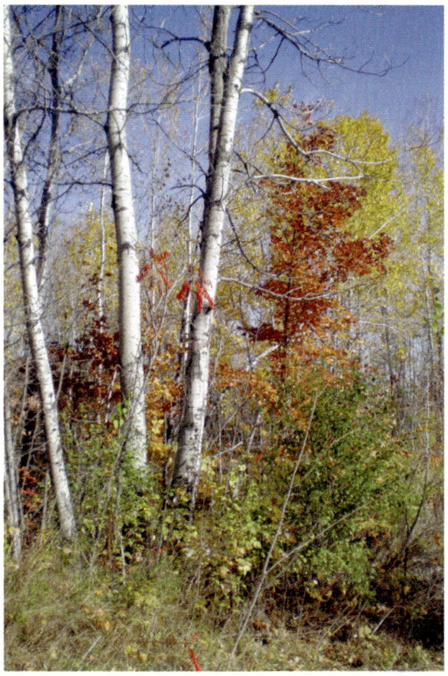

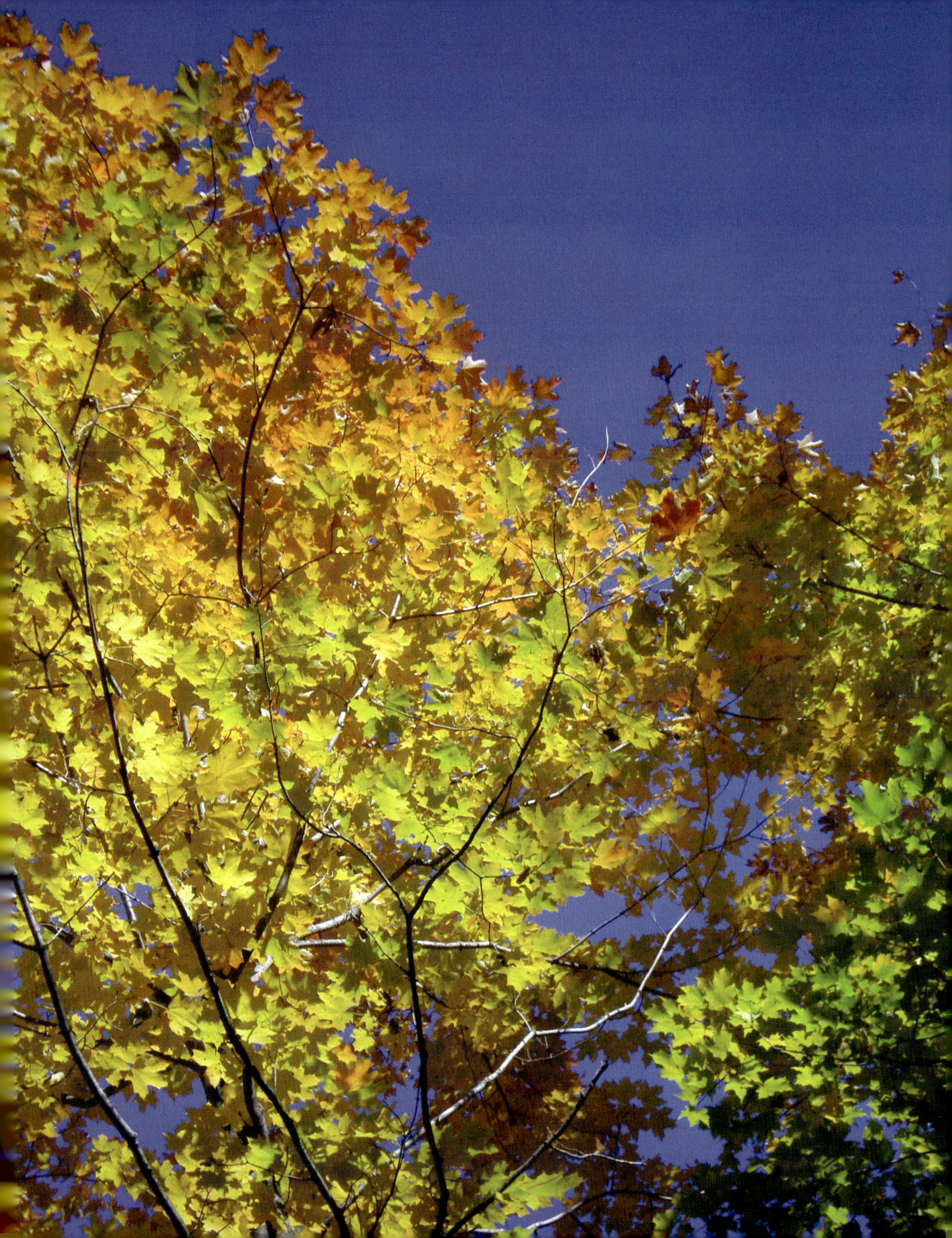

Eau Claire Dells Segment
Marathon County

This portion of the trail goes through a county park that has been beloved by generations, particularly for its waterfall and rocky ledges. The boulders that rise from the river make sunny perches for watching the water flow or for a summer swim. Indeed, the park is so well-loved by area residents, it's a safe guess that many visitors don't even know that the Ice Age Trail goes through the park.

The Eau Claire Dells Segment makes a nice outing for a day or a few days, as the county park, which is open from May through October, contains a playground, picnic area, restrooms, and water. A swimming beach and camping are also available.

Continuing about 1½ miles southwest of the park, the trail follows the Eau Claire River. When walking in the summer, you will often catch glimpses of the river through the trees, because the woods are such a verdant green. Walking on a breezy day keeps the mosquitoes at bay. Otherwise be prepared with bug spray. If you're lucky, you may find a few wild raspberries to eat. If you're really lucky, you'll spot a blue heron flying low over the water looking for fish to catch.

Benches are thoughtfully placed at particularly scenic points overlooking the river. A set of stairs will take you down to the river, where the path is smooth and easy to follow. Both the steps and the trailside benches were made by Eagle Scouts. At this point on the trail, where the steps descend to the river, the Ice Age Trail crosses the 45th parallel. This is the halfway point between the North Pole and the Equator. The trail continues to follow the river for about three-quarter miles until veering slightly to the east for a quarter-mile before reaching County Road Z, at which point the trail becomes a road connector walk.

Directions:

From Wausau take State Highway 29 east to the Hatley/County Highway Y exit. Take County Highway Y north 9.5 miles. At Sportsman Drive, which is a gravel road, turn right and go east 0.3 miles to the trailhead on the north side of the road. You may also continue north on County Highway Y to the Dells of the Eau Claire County Park, which contains ample parking.

Parking:

Limited roadside parking on Sportsman Drive and also on County Road Z, where the trail crosses the road about one mile south and one-half mile west of the park.

Ice Age Trail Adventure
Eau Claire Dells

This was the section of the Ice Age Trail that got Kris hooked on walking the trail. As you walk this segment, you will notice the roots of the yellow birch trees – they look almost like a large bird's foot. We were fascinated to see that the birch trees seemed to grow out of trunks of pine trees. As we discovered later, birch trees often take root in trunks of fallen pine trees.

The day we walked, Sylvia's husband Gene had dropped us off about 3 miles southwest of the park and we walked through woods and onto the banks of the Eau Claire River. Most of the walk was fairly even and gentle. As we crossed a footbridge near the southwest end of the county park, the walk became a bit more strenuous with rocks and some uphill walking, but it was easily accomplished. Allow a bit of extra time if walking with young children.

What I discovered that day, when I first ventured onto the Ice Age Trail, was that I had also found the perfect walking buddy. We walk at a similar pace, and we also enjoy taking time to stop and look at details like flowers and butterflies. We both take pictures whenever we spot something photo-worthy – which, on the Ice Age Trail, is often!

For us, this is a trail to be savored. We tend to walk anywhere from five to twelve miles in a day. We've done more and we've done less. We prefer taking our time, stopping to examine interesting plants, insects, birds, and wildlife. Did you know that dragonflies are called mosquito hawks because they eat so many mosquitoes? Another reason to love these vividly colored insects with the extravagant wings that make them look like miniature helicopters.

– Kris

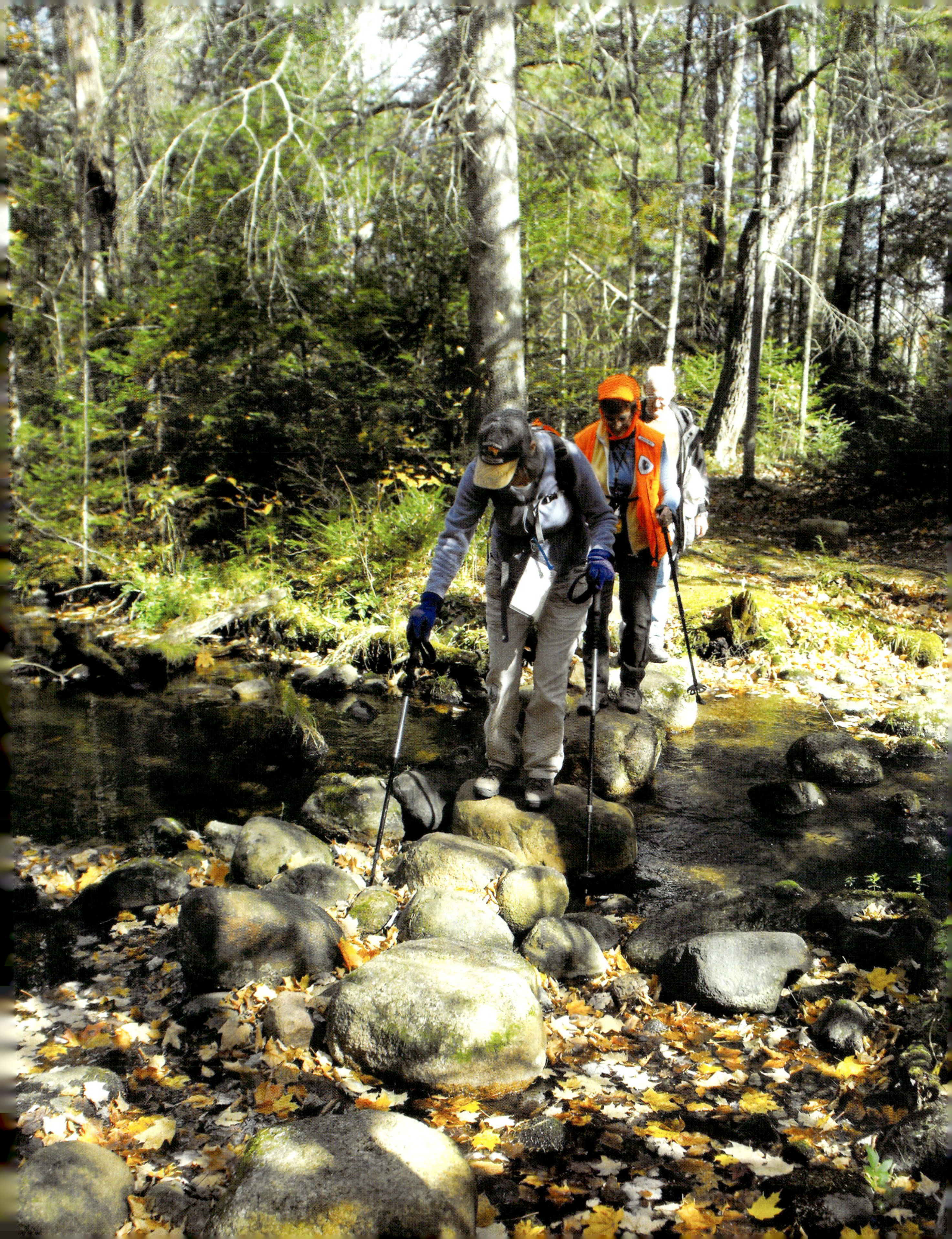

You Go Ahead, I'll Wait

I am one of the Sitting People.
I rest here where the river, no more than a creek,
pushes against my side, then flows past me.
You place your hands against my smooth cheek,
lean your whole body against my solid girth.
I feel the pulse of magma at Earth's molten core,
the flow of lava, like a river deep beneath me.
The cadence of time measured in eons, not minutes,
hours, days, years, nor even centuries.
I rest here, worn smooth by long-ago tumbling
in the river of ice that carried me here.
I remember the mammoth browsing
long before the two-leggeds came along.
Not until the earth buckles again
and chasms open will I move again.
Go. Make your way through the woods.
Your companions are waiting for you
farther up the trail. Come back with a picnic
in the spring when the water rushes past me.
I'll be here. Sitting. Waiting. Still.

– Kris

Belmont, Emmons, Hartman Creek Segments
Portage and Waupaca Counties

Waupaca's Chain O'Lakes resort area brings thousands of visitors and summer residents each year. A premier attraction for the Chain O'Lakes area is Hartman Creek State Park. The Ice Age Trail passes through Hartman Creek State Park, which contains a picturesque loop, and continues through Emmons Creek State Fishery and Wildlife Area to the south.

This segment of the trail is a frequent site for the annual Hike-A-Thon, held on the first Saturday in October and jointly hosted by the Portage and Waupaca County Chapters of the Ice Age Trail Alliance. The chapter volunteers try to highlight a different segment each year and offer various options, generally four, eight or ten miles, or you can walk a shorter distance if you prefer. Apples and water are available at monitor stations set up along the route and refreshments are served after the hike.

Chapter members work hard to get items for door prizes for hikers, most of which are donated by area businesses or individuals who support the trail. Pledges are not necessary but are encouraged, as proceeds from the hike are used locally for development and protection of the trail.

Another popular location for the Hike-A-Thon is the Iola Winter Sports Area with its network of cross country ski trails. The Ice Age Trail also traverses this area, and a sunny winter day is perfect for an Ice Age Trail adventure.

Directions:

To Hartman Creek State Park:
From Waupaca, take State Highway 54 west for 5 miles. The trailhead and parking are on the north side of the highway. To get to the park, turn left on Hartman Creek Road, which is about 1/3 mile east of the trailhead. Go south about 1.5 miles to reach the park.

To Iola Winter Sports Club, Norseman Hill, County Highway MM, Iola: From Stevens Point, take Highway 10 east to Highway 161. Travel east on Highway 161. Turn left (north) on County Highway A. Turn right on County Highway MM and continue 3.5 miles to the Iola Winter Sports Area.

Meeting Chapter Members
Hike-A-Thon Welcomes Visitors for Fall Colors

Each chapter of the Ice Age Trail organizes several events throughout the year, ranging from spring flower hikes to field trips and work days. Group hikes are open to all and may be on foot or on snowshoes. Ruth Sommers, one of the thousand-milers, met her trail-walking buddy, Dianne Genz, when she attended a snowshoe hike on the Ice Age Trail.

For several years, Kris has joined the Hike-A-Thon and reveled in the glory of autumn in Wisconsin. Crunching along a path strewn with brown oak leaves, looking up to see a maple dressed in crimson or gold, and sharing the day with other trail enthusiasts of all ages – it's all part of the annual Hike-A-Thon hosted by the Waupaca and Portage County Chapters. The hike takes place regardless of rain, snow, or sun.

The weekend of the Hike-A-Thon coincides with the annual Hidden Studios Tour, Art along the Ice Age Trail, a tour of working studios in Central Wisconsin. The three-day tour has become a weekend destination for many groups and complements the Hike-A-Thon with the opportunity to meet nearby artists and watch them

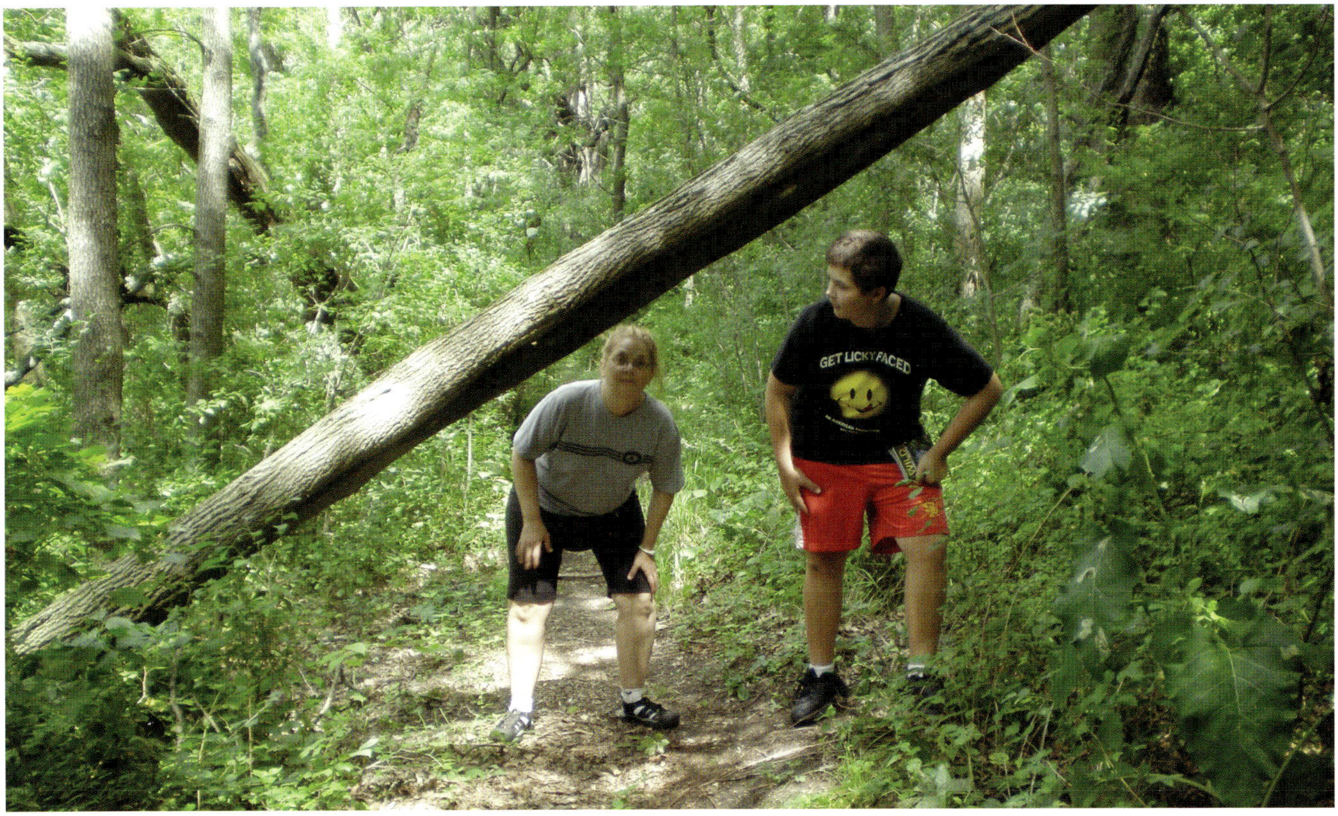
GET LICKYFACED

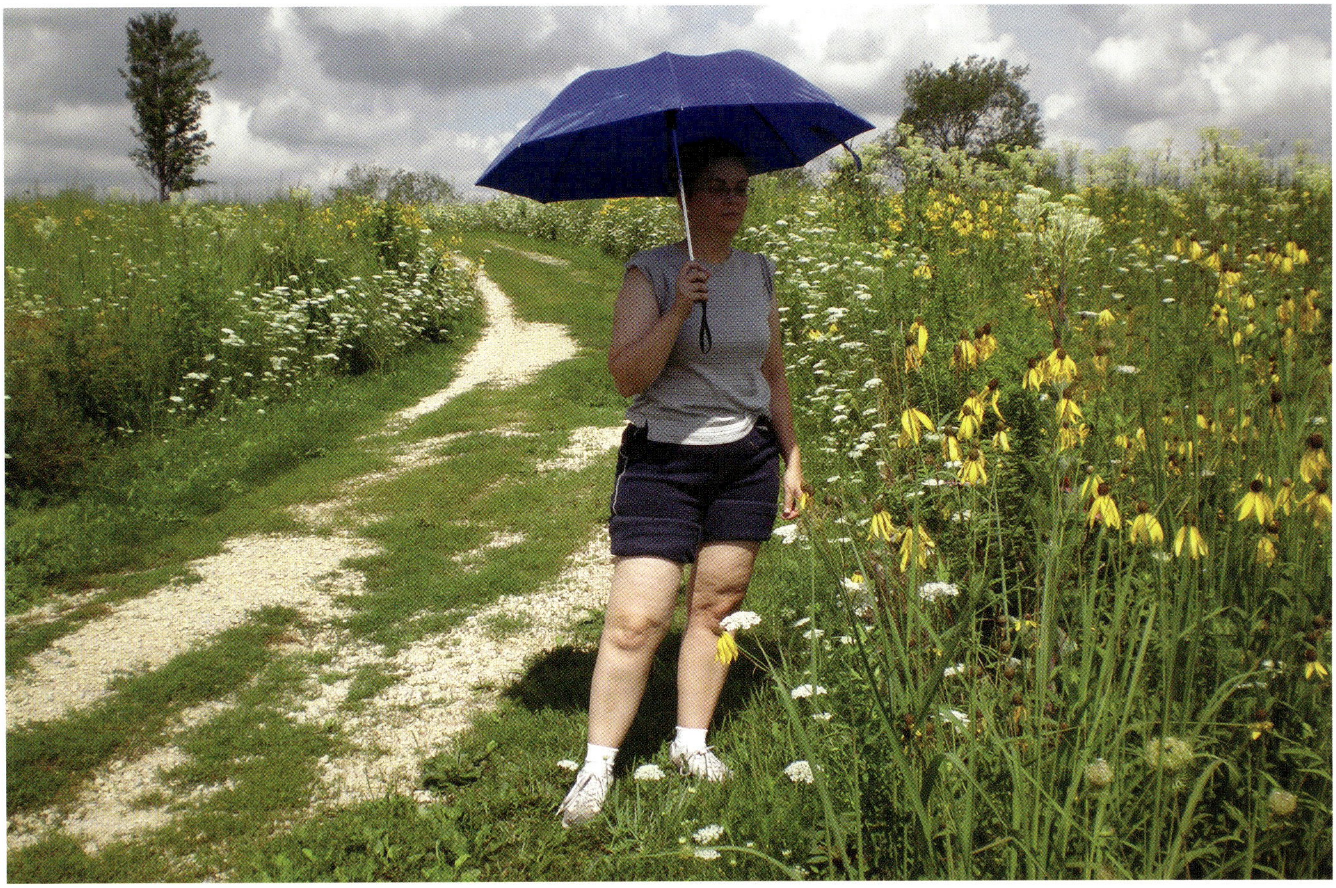

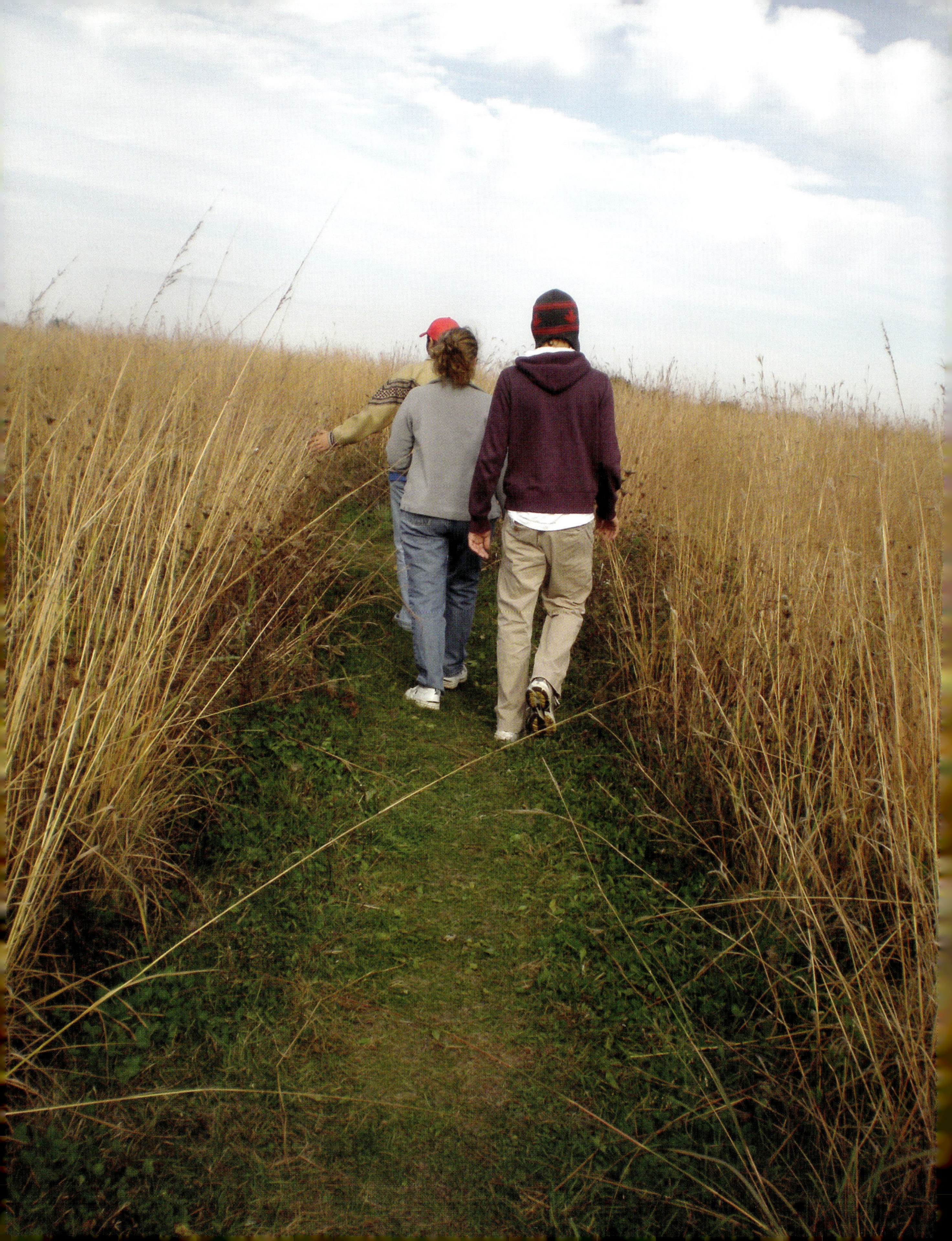

at work. For more information, including a map of the participating studios, go to www.HiddenStudiosArtTour.com

Sylvia and Kris braved the cold on a January day to walk the Ice Age Trail through the Iola Winter Sports Complex. Fortunately, the trail crossed county roads frequently, giving us opportunities to meet our driver and warm up in the car for a bit before continuing on. As several other ski trails share this recreational area, it's important to watch for the yellow blazes on trees and signposts.

A thermos of hot chocolate does wonders to revive chilly fingers and toes, and many nearby communities boast cafes and coffee shops with homemade soups, creative sandwiches, and decadent desserts.

– Kris

January on the Ice Age Trail

Cardinals become grace notes
random red decorations in pines.
As we walk through the snow-filled
path in the forest we are grateful—
someone has gone before us,
forming a flattened crust with snowshoes.
We step lightly, flat-footed,
like tightrope walkers above the deep.

– Kris

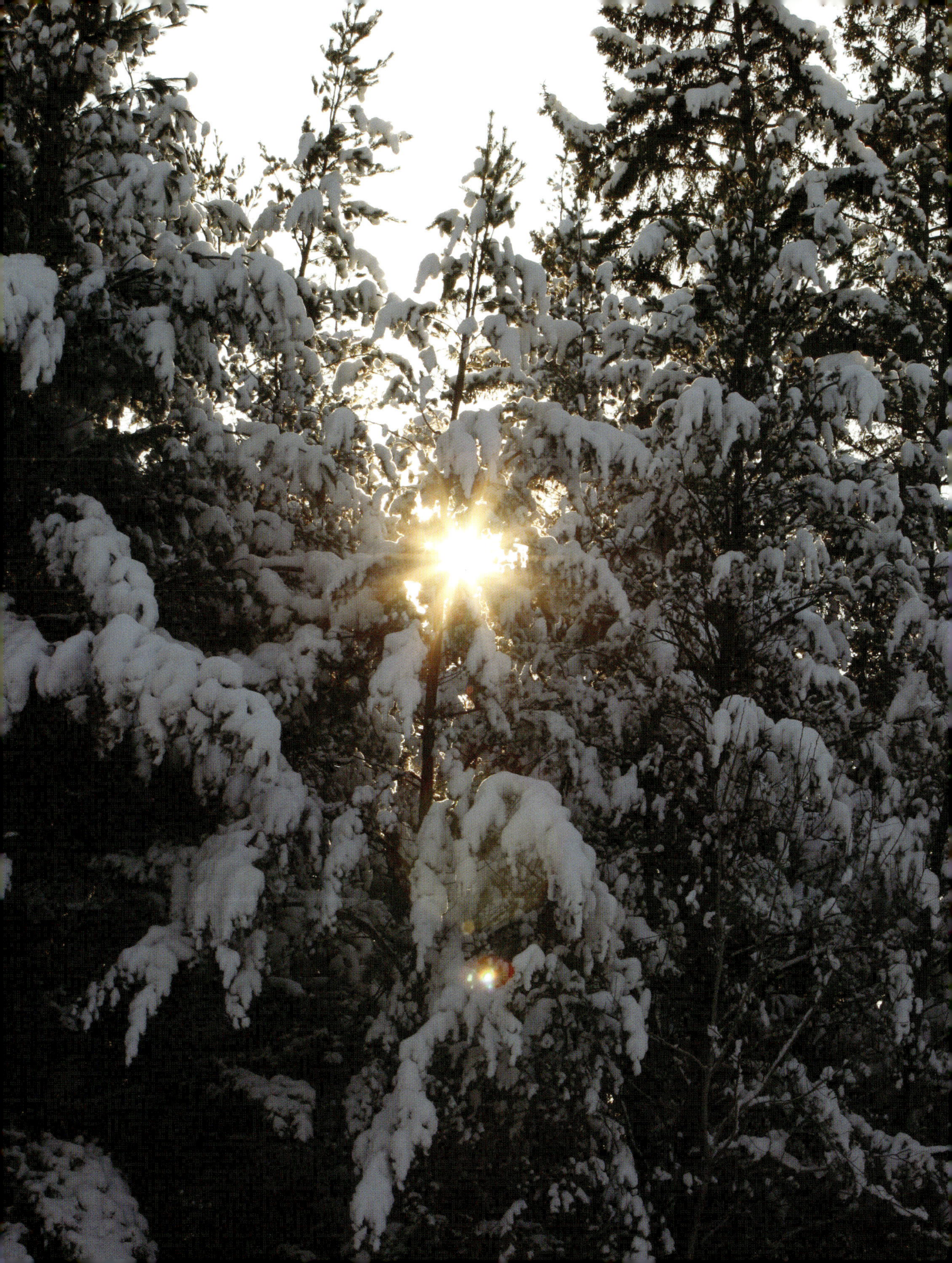

A New Angle

While hiking the Ice Age Trail in Waushara County, I thought about fishing. On a path more than a hundred feet above the Mecan River, I looked down on what is known as one of the best trout streams in Central Wisconsin. It looked so inviting I thought, "I'll have to get myself a fishing license again this year." I laughed as I remembered an announcement on the radio last year offering fishing lessons for women. I had shouted back at it, " Wisconsin women know how to fish! We've always fished!"

My mom taught us how to thread a worm on the hook and catch pan fish and at an early age. She didn't have a stringer so she'd just take a branchy twig and put it through the gills. Then we'd take our sunfish or crappie home to fry. We had the fun of cleaning little shiners and pulling out their small, bubble-like air sacs intact. I once thought all fish had that little balloon and needed it to float.

I'll never forget fishing in Pike Lake where I caught a prize crappie. The men at the boathouse said "Oh" and "Ah" and praised it immensely. That made me a very proud eleven-year-old girl. What did we do with the crappie? We ate it, of course. These days, my son John, an avid fisherman, has prize fish like that mounted.

One year the women in our homemakers club took a group of nursing home patients for a fishing day at Otter Lake (a lake very near the Ice Age Trail). It was a good time even if "Old Whiskers" wheelchair rolled into the water a few inches. He had a big smile and could still beat me putting a worm on the hook. And how we laughed that time daughter Marie taught her boyfriend to bait a hook. My! How squeamish he acted.

This spring I'm telling John and my brother Fred that we are going trout fishing. I've read the Department of Natural Resources is stocking more than 615,000 catchable trout by the opening date of the inland trout season. Brown, rainbow and brook trout will be delivered to the streams. Some will be included for clinics and kids' fishing in small lakes and ponds. I've had little experience with trout, but know it's quite an art because trout put up a good fight when hooked. I'll need my license, a booklet of trout regulations, and the regular manual titled "Go Fish."

Pulling up a wiggling fish or catching a frog will make a kid's day. For adults, there's the outside air, relaxation, and the soothing sound of water. So just get prepared and let "Mom" take you fishing this spring or ice fishing in the winter.

– Sylvia

Mourning Cloak

Yellow Swallowtail

Butterflies: Flowers that fly and all but sing.
– Robert Frost

Spring Morning and the Mourning Cloak

Dark butterflies with yellow-fringed wings flitted above the melting snow as I hiked along the Ice Age Trail. "A mature butterfly in early spring?" I thought. "It can't be true." But, after a bit of homework, I found I had seen a Mourning Cloak butterfly. The facts about the Mourning Cloak proved most interesting, too.

Its scientific name is Nymphalis Antiopa. The common name Mourning Cloak comes from the Germanic languages and it could make one think of a cloak. It was sometimes called the butterfly with a petticoat. In England it's called the Camberwell Beauty. I'd say that's a better name for these graceful gliders with the 62 to 75 mm wingspans.

In Northern areas where it overwinters, the unmated adults mate and lay eggs in the spring. Later, the larvae feed on the tree sap of willows, aspen, cottonwood, and hackberry. The Mourning Cloak is one of our longest-lived butterflies. Some live from seven months to a year. They overwinter under fallen trees and you may see them on warm spring days even though patches of snow cover the ground.

So, next time you see this dark-winged butterfly with the petticoat, know that it's the Mourning Cloak. What a welcome sight flying in the warm spring air!

– Sylvia

Monarch

Milbert's Tortoiseshell and Fritillary

Monarch

Monarch

Fritillary

Yellow Sulphur butterflies

Deerfield Segment
Waushara County
**Mourning Cloak in April
(Butterfly over-winters)**

Options:

3.7 miles: Exit 131 off I-39 at County Road V, Village of Hancock. Take County Road V east to Ice Age Trail parking on Beechnut Drive. Walk to County Road O

6 miles: For longer hike, from Hancock take County Road B south to Bohn Lake parking site. From Bohn Lake walk northeast to County Road O

Portage Canal Segment
Columbia County

The historic city of Portage takes its name from its description as "le portage" by the French fur traders. Located on a marshy floodplain between the Wisconsin and the Fox Rivers, Portage served as a natural connection between the two rivers and was a center of trade and commerce. A canal was built in the 1800s to facilitate trade along the two rivers. A bicycle path now runs along the old canal, which is no longer in use.

Southwest of Portage, the Ice Age Trail follows Levee Road along the Wisconsin River, which runs through the Pine Island State Wildlife Area for several miles. Crossing the bridge on Highway 33 into Portage, one finds scenic Pauquette Park – an inviting spot for a picnic.

The home of writer Zona Gale has been preserved by the Women's Civic League of Portage and is open for tours. Gale was the first woman to win the Pulitzer Prize for drama in 1921. Another notable citizen who called the Portage area home was naturalist John Muir, who founded the Sierra Club. As a boy, he lived with his family on a farm near Portage.

Today, the downtown features quaint shops with tasty refreshments for trail-walkers, including popcorn and an ice cream parlor. Continue walking through town to complete your adventure at the Indian Agency House, alongside the old canal. Built in 1832, it is one of Wisconsin's earliest homes. It was built by the U.S. government as a residence for John Kinzie, the first Indian agent to the Ho-Chunk, and is now open for tours.

Directions:

Levee Road Connecting Route:

From Portage, take State Highway 33 south, crossing the Wisconsin River. Turn right on Fairfield Street, one-quarter mile south of the bridge. Within a mile, Fairfield Street becomes Levee Road. Continue 7.1 miles to Schepp Road. Walk back to Portage along the road or the levee that runs between the road and the Wisconsin River. (The area may be flooded in the spring.)

Portage Canal Segment:

2.8 miles

Begin at Pauquette Park at State Highway 33 just north of the Wisconsin River. Walk a block south to Edgewater Street and go east about a mile to Mullett Street, for approximately another mile; and then veer north on Agency House Road, walking north a little over a mile to the Agency House Road trailhead. You may also look for the yellow Ice Age Trail blazes through the city. On Edgewater Street an optional spur crosses the canal and follows the Wisconsin River for about one-half mile.

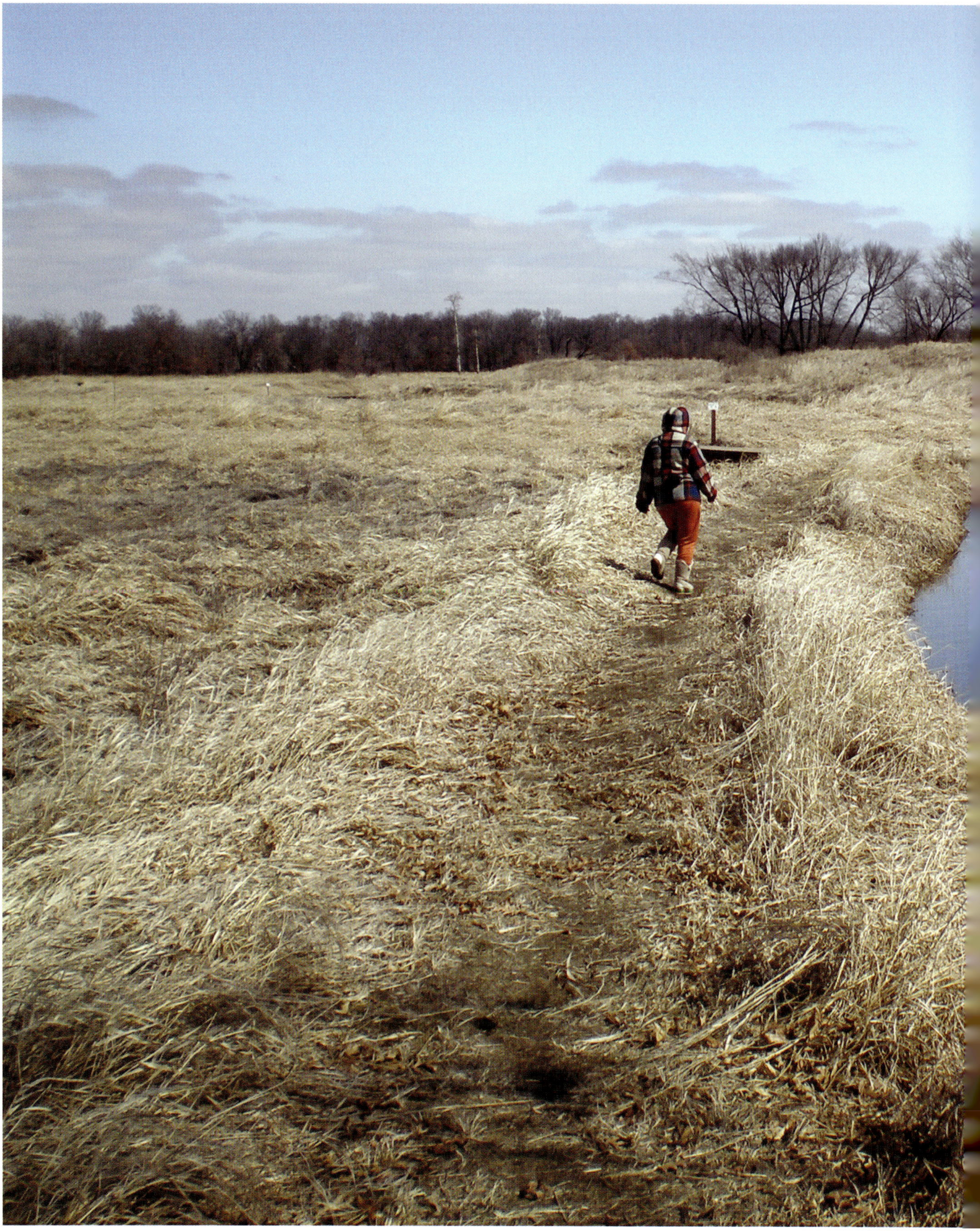

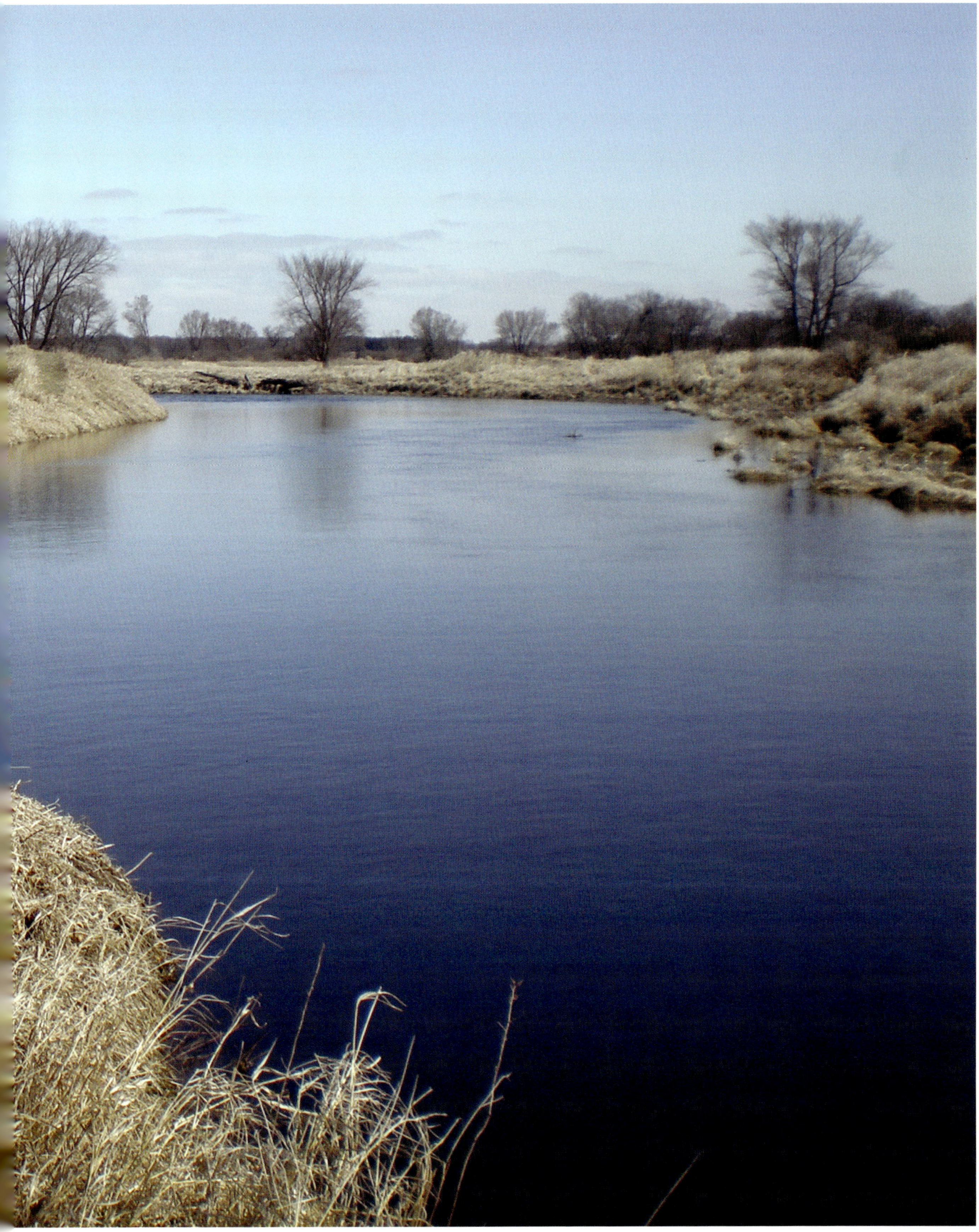

Walking through Portage

Although both the levee walk and the walk through Portage may be easily accomplished in one day, the quaint charm of this historic city invites an overnight stay. The day we walked both segments, the Wisconsin River and Levee Road were just beginning a spring awakening, and we spotted a variety of migratory birds including Canadian Geese and Sandhill Cranes. Designated a Wisconsin Rustic Road, Levee Road is lightly traveled, and walking on the levee brought us even closer to the river. An optional side trip to the Pine Island Savanna features several native species of trees such as oak, red and white pine, silver maple, and river birch, interspersed with sand prairie, containing many species of wildflowers.

As we walked through Portage, we chose to walk along the Wisconsin River for a bit longer, and then walk along the canal before turning to the north to rejoin the trail. In doing so, we missed our driver, Gene, who became increasingly concerned when he didn't see us cross the road where he was waiting. When we didn't see him as we walked past the downtown, we assumed he was napping or listening to a Brewers game on the car radio and simply too distracted to see us. We kept walking northeast, following the Portage Canal, eventually finishing at the Indian Agency House.

We were dismayed when we did not see Gene waiting for us at the trailhead. At that time, Sylvia was proud of being able to find her way on the trail without relying upon a cellphone or a GPS. We later learned that Gene had tried to call Kris's cellphone earlier in the afternoon, only to hear it ringing behind him in her purse, which she'd left in the back seat of the car. "A lot of good that does me," he'd thought. We later learned he'd even called the hospital emergency room to see if we'd been involved in an accident.

Fortunately, the caretaker at the Indian Agency House was outside working on some early spring yard work, and he kindly allowed us to use his cellphone. Ironically we did not know the number for the car's Onstar phone, so it took several additional calls to family in Thorp and Arpin to track down the number. As we weren't carrying pen or pencil, we used a stick to scratch the phone number in the dirt when a relative eventually called back with the number. By now the caretaker must have thought we were totally inept, because he graciously offered to drive us back into Portage to meet Gene, who was relieved to see us. The day's adventure was a good reminder for us to be more explicit about our directions and our back-up plans for meeting (as well as convincing us to carry a cellphone while walking).

– Kris

Devil's Lake Segment
Sauk County

A most impressive example of glacial activity can be seen on this segment of the Ice Age Trail. The Wisconsin River cut a gorge through the quartzite rock of the Baraboo Range, 500-foot high quartzite bluffs. Melt water from the glacier filled the gorge and a moraine formed at each end of the valley creating Devil's Lake. It is believed this happened in a short period of time making this a unique feature and the deepest lake in Wisconsin.

The rocks of the quartzite bluffs are giant size and can weigh many tons. Many of these rocks have a neat purple hue and look like huge sculptures jutting out on the ridge. Some special rocks have names like Balanced Rock and Devil's Doorway.

The view from the top is awesome! Hikers will be high above Devil's Lake and looking toward the Baraboo Hills beyond. These hills are approximately 1.6 billion years old and are thought to have once been taller than the Rocky Mountains.

On spring days May flowers grow beside the trail. Lady breeches, bloodroot, and hepatica are plentiful. Pine trees, wildlife, and turkey vultures can be seen all times of the year. There are interesting side trips, effigy mounds and a nature center in the park. A side trip to the International Crane Foundation near Baraboo will add to your walk any day.

This will be very steep hiking. So choose a nice day, pack a lunch, and take stops to rest on the way up or down.

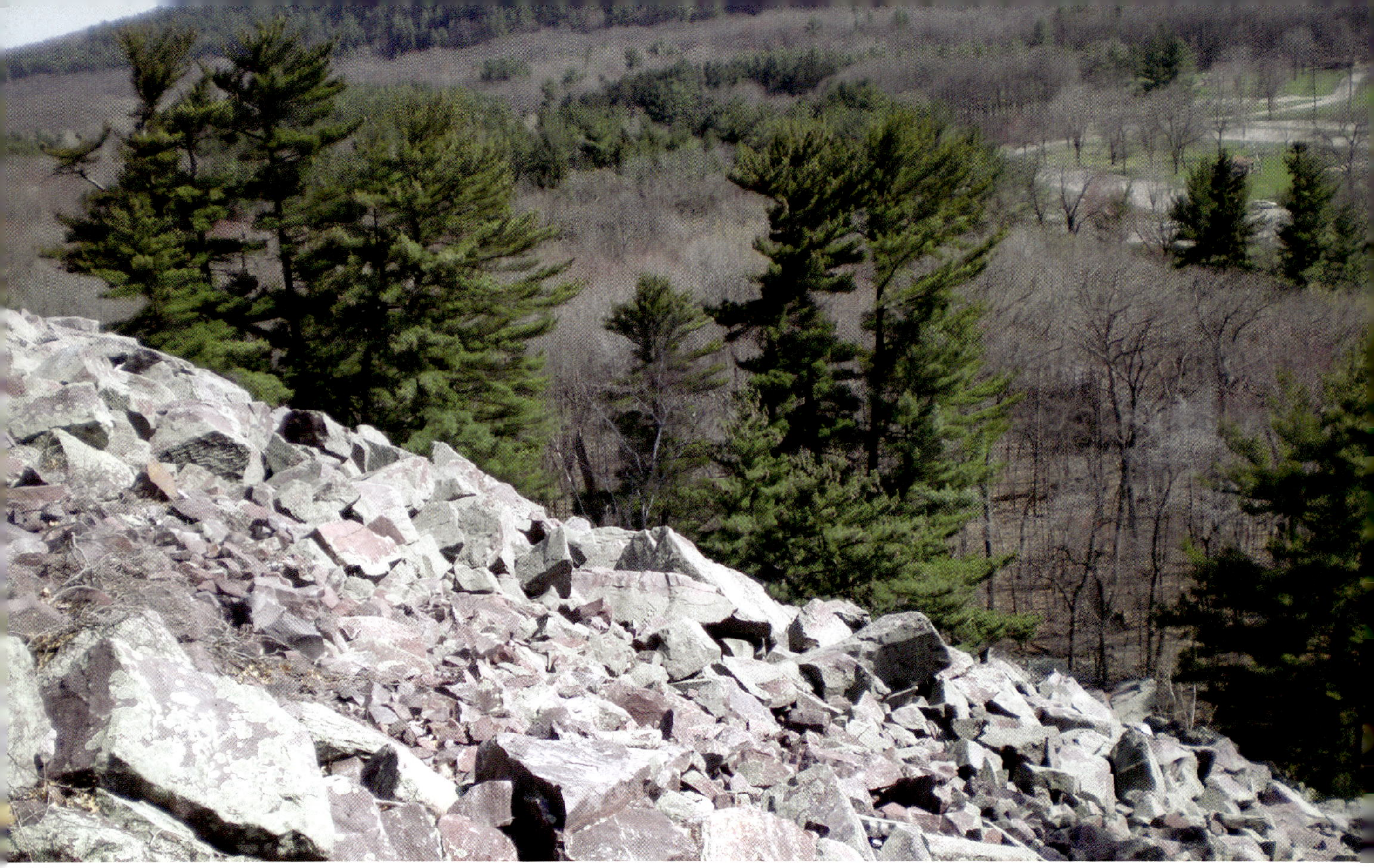

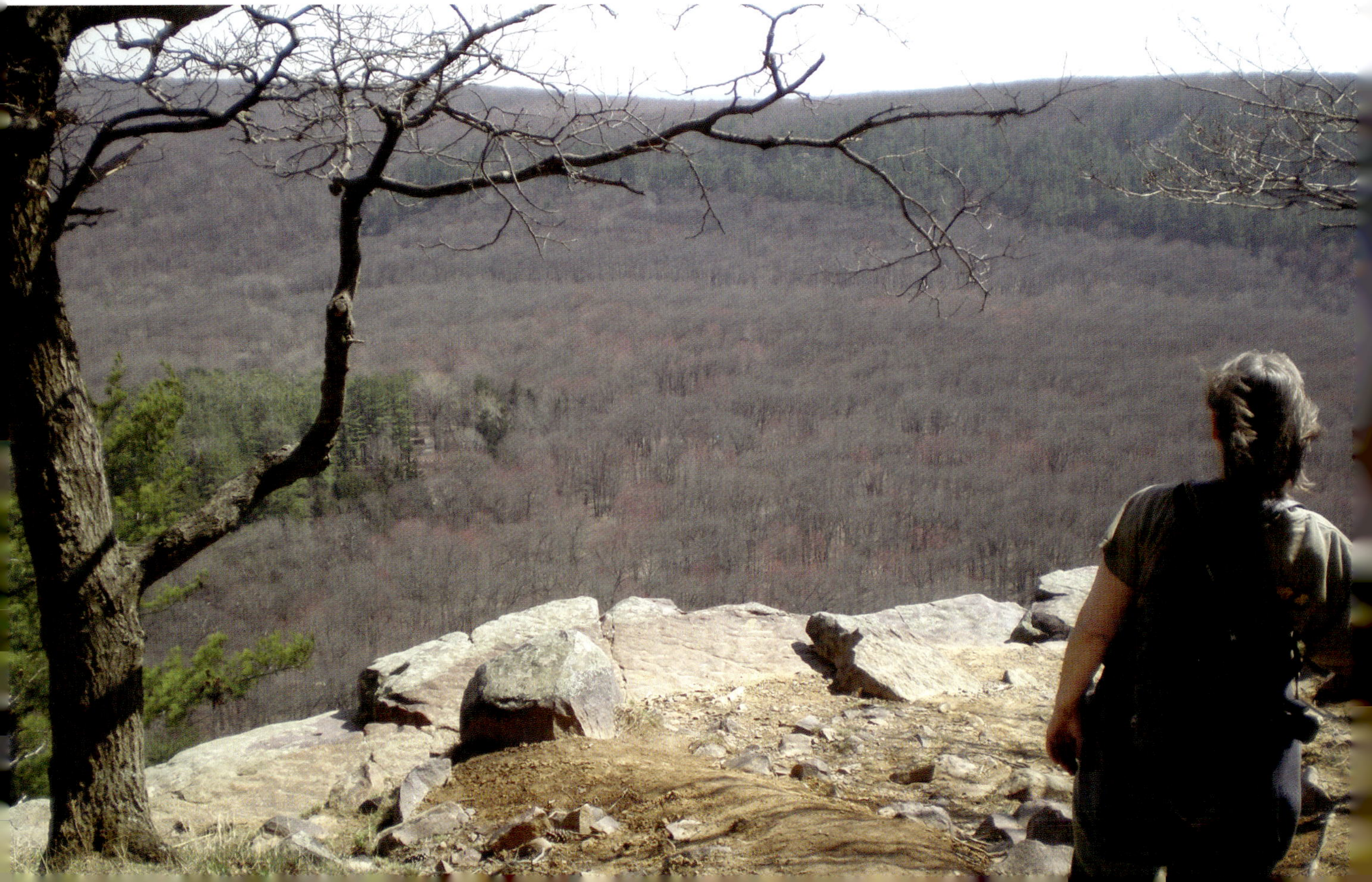

Options:

3 miles: From parking lot on the north end of the lake, in Devil's Lake State Park near South Lake Road to south parking lot.

A shorter hike uphill in the park and hike back down gives good view of quartzite rocks and lake below.

1.5 miles: Northeast of lake, parking lot near Tower Road, trail crosses County Road DL. Hike to lake.

4 miles: From parking lot just off State Highway 113, hike to north tip of lake.

Merrimac Ferry: Highway 113 to Marsh Road, take ferry across Wisconsin River.

4.4 miles: Merrimac Segment: Marsh Road northwest of Merrimac to South Lake Drive on Devil's Lake

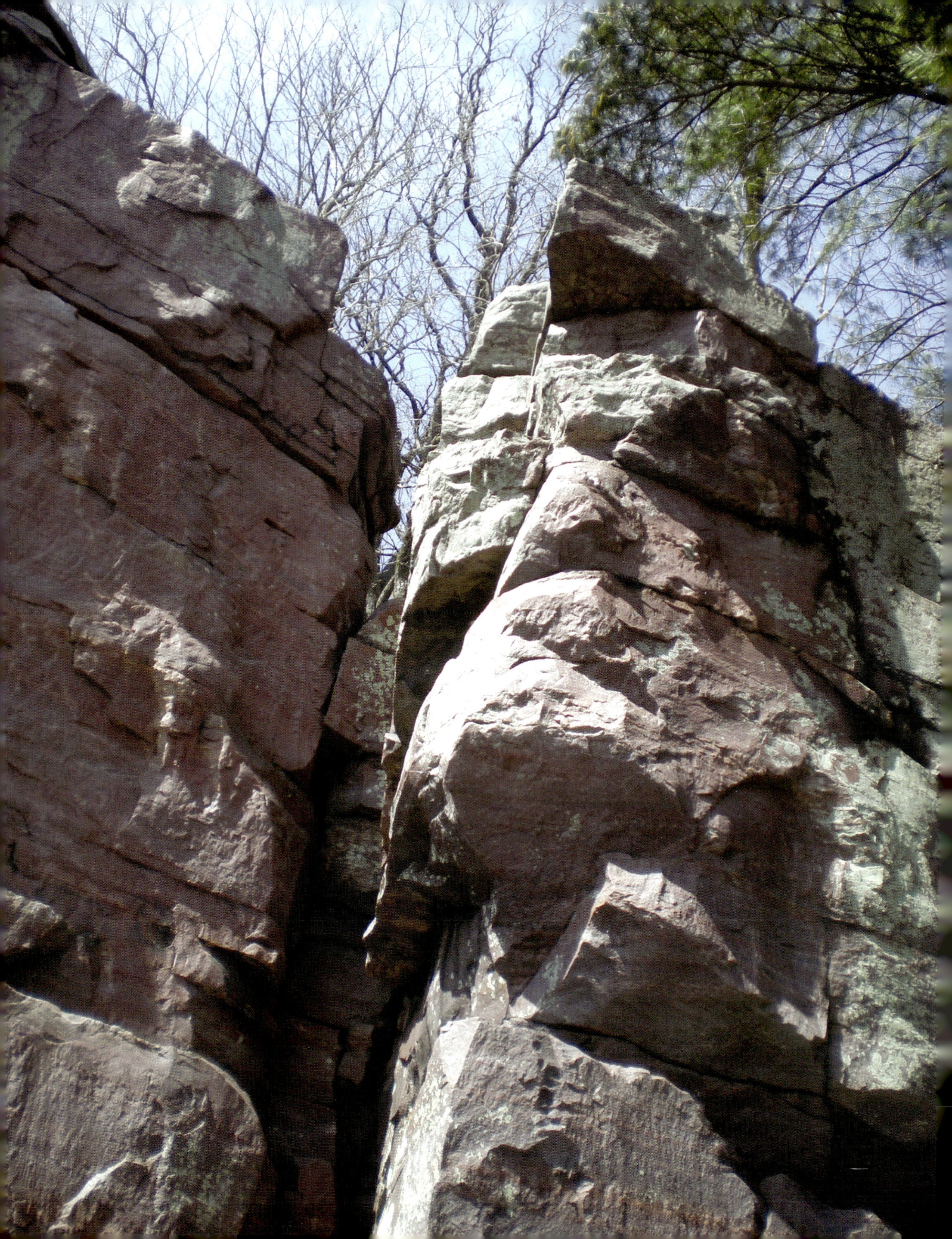

Those Vipers

It was a fresh spring day with trees budding and new plants sprouting up for their first rays of sun. We had a pleasant hike up the hill at Devil's Lake State Park and spent some time enjoying the scenic view. It was on the way down the rocky trail, when I stepped with triple speed scraping my legs on the boulders covering the rocky hillside above Devil's Lake. Calling out to my companion hiker that I'd just heard a rattlesnake, I flew past her almost out of breath. She laughed and told me it was only a bird. I just couldn't quite believe it. I knew she didn't share my feelings about snakes. Especially evident on an earlier trek in Waupaca County when I saw her stop and ask a big pine snake if it liked warming itself in the spring sunshine.

Through the years, I've tried to change my attitude and look at beneficial side of these creatures. I know that Wisconsin has few poisonous snakes. The timber and the massasauga rattlesnakes are the only snakes listed in that category. The latter is a protected species, and found in only certain parts of the state. Most snakes here are harmless and feed on small rodents, frogs and bugs. So I improved my outlook. When students brought in a garter snake or a grass snake I'd pretend to like it.

One day, a 6th grade boy asked if he could bring

his sister's snake to school. Of course, I said yes. What a surprise! The sister was dressed in white go-go boots, short skirt, and wore a sparkling comb in her hair. Over her shoulders she carried an eight-and-a-half foot boa constrictor! It stretched around her waist and across the front of the classroom with Howard holding "Agnew's" tail.

The student gave a good science report telling how the boa ate rodents and how it was able to swallow its prey. Just the same, I breathed a sigh of relief when they left. And it pleased me that my principal didn't mind my science presenter, an exotic dancer who loved to dance with Agnew around her neck!

I never dreamed that three years later on the 8th grade trip to the Minneapolis Zoo, I would see "Agnew the Boa" again. That long snake was coiled around a tree in the reptile house. My student's sister had retired from exotic dancing and donated her boa to the zoo. Agnew, the snake, looked much better to me in that setting.

But going back to that day in the spring on the Ice Age Trail near Devil's Lake, I must tell you we stopped at a nearby restaurant at the foot of the hill. I asked the owner if rattlesnakes were ever seen on the rocky hills. "Oh yes," he said. "I had a couple of hikers in here last year that were really shook up after seeing a rattlesnake on that very hill."

Just a bird, huh? Well, Maybe. I love the Ice Age Trail with its woods and walks. I'll stay on the trail and not disturb the unknown. I'll respect all the wildlife, breathe the fresh air, and keep on hiking.

– Sylvia

Turkey Vultures on Spirit Lake

Joggers overtake us easily
as we struggle up the path.
We have walked nine miles
today and are tired, but still
we trudge. Even the cement
path here is old, so old.
At last, a look-out, sheltered by pines,
the lake's mirrored surface far below.
We look straight out – eye-to-eye
with the eagle-sized birds.
They do not cry out, but circle--
in silence they circle.

– Kris

Cranes: Least and Most in Wisconsin

I heard their call, rushed out, looked skyward to see a pair of Sandhill Cranes heading toward our wetland. Minutes later, a second pair followed flying high above me. After a winter that just wouldn't quit, I welcomed this sign of spring.

Sandhills are the most abundant crane species in the world. Wisconsin is home to a great many of them. But did you know Wisconsin is also the home of the rarest species of crane, the Whooping Crane? Both species have interesting stories in their past.

In the 1930s Aldo Leopold reported Sandhhll Cranes down to 25 breeding pairs in Wisconsin. Now, they are common here and I've enjoyed watching that first pair for the last three years. They surprised me last year strutting up and down our corn field protecting three rusty brown chicks. Sandhills have a red cap, mate for life, and usually lay two eggs. So my pair is special!

Wisconsin is also home to Whooping Cranes, the most rare of the 15 crane species. Now since I'm a birder-hiker, I made a visit to the International Crane Foundation near Baraboo, Wisconsin. It was fun to take photos of two free roaming Whoopers on the 100 acre restored prairie and wetland. Success with my camera took a while because the big birds kept their beaks in the water searching for amphibians.

In 1941 Whooping Cranes numbered only 22 individual birds in the world. Today, thanks to reintroduction, 100 cranes are surviving. It's not a large number, but progress has been made since they were in danger of becoming extinct.

In 1982, one man spent 15 hours a day for six

weeks with a Whooper just to get it to lay an egg. The egg was fertilized by artificial insemination and when incubators didn't work, Sandhill Cranes were used to hatch the Whooping Crane chicks.

In 1999, the International Crane Foundation decided to create a new flock of Whooping Cranes that would migrate between Wisconsin and Florida. The cranes were trained to follow an ultralight aircraft to Florida. To keep the cranes from imprinting on humans, all trainers and even the pilots wore crane costumes. So far, some young cranes and older birds have successfully migrated. But it has not been an easy task.

The refuge is an educational place when it comes to cranes. In the exhibit pod you can view cranes from Japan, Siberia, Australia and Africa. My favorites were the Japanese Cranes with their beaks pointed straight up calling in unison.

That took me back to the year Miss Dori Eto visited our school from Japan. She was here to translate our children's literature into Japanese. In return, she taught us about ancient crane stories and myths. Cranes are a sign of peace and luck in Japan.

She also told us a more recent story about radiation after the atomic bomb. People in her country folded origami cranes for a little Japanese girl to help her get well. If she received 1000 cranes, she believed she would live. And it worked.

Our students folded colored paper cranes all semester. We carefully hid them in a classroom closet. On the day of Miss Dori's going away party, the children surprised her with a chain of 1,000 cranes in appreciation of her wonderful stories. There were happy tears that day.

So when it comes to cranes, Wisconsin is home to the most and the least. Sandhills are in abundance now, and hunting is allowed, though that makes a bit of controversy. The number of the Whooping Cranes is up to 100 now and growing. So get out and enjoy listening and viewing. Join the crane count every April. Or make a visit to the International Crane Foundation to enjoy a day hike and view some Whoopers!

Interesting Side Trip
Devil's Lake, Sauk County Segment

The International Crane Foundation is located between Baraboo and Wisconsin Dells just off Highway 12

International Crane Foundation
E 11376 Shady Lane Rd.
Baraboo, WI 53913

The International Crane Foundation is dedicated to saving the world's cranes by research, education and reintroduction. Home to Whooping Cranes, Sandhill Cranes and several international species of crane.

Open April to October 31

Walking trail for viewing

Restored Prairie
Dane County

One of the best sights to see is the prairie in full bloom. It was a sea of color as I hiked along the oak savanna and prairie grasslands of Dane County. Butterflies flitted happily around Queen Anne's lace, black-eyed Susan, and milkweed. Swallowtail butterflies flew in the breeze above purple coneflowers. I saw a field of wonderful plants growing and blossoming all the way to the horizon.

One of my uncles once said, "There are no weeds, only God's plants." I thought that saying was just right when I saw the prominence of Queen Anne's lace growing on that prairie. Some people call this plant "carrot weed." Queen Anne's lace is a common plant in fields and open areas and was introduced to us from Europe. The carrots we eat today were once cultivated from this beautiful flowering plant. It is a biennial plant that grows four feet tall with fern-like leaves and tiny white flowers. The flowers form a cluster that reminds one of a lace doily.

One legend says this lacy flower is named after Queen Anne of England who had her ladies in waiting making lace. Another says the queen herself was the lace maker and when she pricked her finger a single drop of blood fell into the lace and made the dark purple floret in the center. Also, it's interesting to note that Caroline Kennedy didn't look at this plant as just a weed. She loved the plant so much she ordered some Queen Anne's lace for her wedding bouquet.

Prairie restoration has been giving us back some of the prairie we have lost. After a special planting, there are plenty of perennial plants that come up year after year providing a very refreshing landscape. No chemicals, no watering, and no weeding to be done. So prairie restoration makes perfect sense. Wisconsin originally had 2.1 million acres of prairie. These acres have declined to 10,000 acres today. So I thank the prairie enthusiasts working to restore these beautiful grasslands that humans and wildlife can enjoy.

The prairie provides a shelter belt, especially for birds. Walking on the prairie, I saw cardinals, turkeys, and a Red-headed Woodpecker. They say the Brown Thrasher and Wood Thrush will be benefitting species, also. I'll be looking for them on a future hike.

On that Dane County prairie hike I saw glacial striations on boulders strewn across the trail. "Striations" is a neat geological term that I am proud to include in my Ice Age Trail vocabulary. Striations are fine scratch marks on rocks with rounded corners. These rocks were worn down from years of travel in the ice of a glacier. We could say they came from Canada via the glacial express. These long distance rock travelers are called erratics. Some made it all the way to Dane County in Southern Wisconsin. I stood on a couple of glacial erratics as I looked over the prairie in bloom. I felt like queen of the field!

– Sylvia

Restored Prairie
Columbia & Dane County

What you may see:

Sections of the Ice Age Trail that include natural or restored prairie are scenic and refreshing. Whether you see a tall sea of grasses or a mixed field of black-eyed Susans and Queen Anne's lace you are certain to enjoy it. Views of prairie from glacial moraines are impressive when you stand above, looking at a vista of peaceful color interspersed with the sound of song birds and soft breezes.

These hikes may bring views of grouse, quail, turkey and more.

For those with a scientific bent there are caterpillars, butterflies, leaf hoppers, and spiders to study.

Occasionally one may come upon a glacial erratic. Glacial erratics are huge stones carried by the glacier many miles from where they started.

Some of them may even have "striations" on them. These are fine scratch marks worn into the huge rocks as they traveled along with the ice.

Options:

1.6 miles: Eastern Lodi Marsh Segment. From Lodi, find parking on Lodi-Springfield Road. This loop has gnarly old oak trees.

2 miles: Near Cross Plains Segment —within Indian Lake Park. Off Highway 19 find Indian Lake County Park for main parking area.

6.8 miles: Verona Segment: Wesner Road to County Road PD (McKee Road) Prairie Moraine County Park

Or to Badger Prairie County Park in Verona: major prairie restoration

Over 200 acres completed

Lapham Peak Segment
Waukesha County

On the Ice Age Trail this section will wind through woods, across open meadows and over restored prairie. Many large white oak trees can be seen. Also, an Indian marker tree points west toward Nemahbin Lake.

Lapham Peak is a glacial-formed kame, a conical hill formed by streams flowing downward through the shafts of ice. The Kettle Moraine has some of the most important kames in the world. Lapham Peak has an interesting history worth reading about. A wooden tower is at the peak and gives one good views of the Kettle Moraine's rolling hills. Looking into the distance you can see Holy Hill and the city of Hartland.

Wildflowers are plentiful. For example, Dutchman's breeches and wild geranium make an appearance in spring. Purple coneflower and evening primrose grow near the trail in summer. In autumn a swishy walk in fallen leaves can be special fun for children and family hikers.

Butterflies, wild turkey, bluebirds, woodpeckers, and wildlife are all good sights on this section. For the person who wants to spend more time, a rest on an Aldo Leopold bench is good, too. It's also a good place to eat your lunch or trail mix.

The city of Delafield has interesting places to visit. It is home to the Lang Company that specializes in calendars, as well as St. John's Northwestern Military Academy and Nashotah House.

Options:

2.5 miles: From I-94 near Delafield, take Exit 285 and go south 1 mile to Lapham Park main entrance. Hike the Ice Age Trail through the park's Kettle Moraine State Forest to parking on Cushing Park Road.

7.8 miles: Cushing Park Road to parking area for the Lapham Peak Unit of the Kettle Moraine State Forest. Follow the Ice Age Trail to the Glacial Drumlin Trail at the UW-Waukesha Field Station

Increase Miles on the Ice Age Trail

"Oh good! Steps," Ruth said as we climbed 120 steps to Lapham Peak, a lofty height located on the Ice Age Trail near Delafield, Wisconsin. We climbed the 45 foot lookout tower with our hair blowing straight up in the cold November wind. Breathless, we reached the top and marveled that we could see far and wide over Nagawicka Lake. In the distance we could see as far as Holy Hill in Washington County.

Lapham Peak is a state park on the Glacial Drumlin State Trail and is named after Increase Lapham. It surprised me to learn he is known as the father of the National Weather Bureau. I had read about Mr. Lapham as an early Wisconsin author (with a strange first name) but hadn't read his important biography. In 1936, he came to Milwaukee to survey city plots and also draw a basic plat of the city.

Increase would climb to the peak, a glacial kame, and observe the weather. He believed weather could be predicted and mapped. Later, he traveled to Washington, D.C., to ask legislators to establish a National Weather Bureau. Today, the park at Lapham Peak offers three picnic areas, a campsite, prairie restoration area, trails for skiing, and biking, and even a trail for dog sled training.

After we had climbed to the peak and back down, a couple living next to the trail invited us for tea. We accepted. I was offered green tea and wondered if I, a coffee-drinker, would like it. To my surprise, it was very refreshing!

Some good humor and stories shared around the table certainly helped make our day. The couple

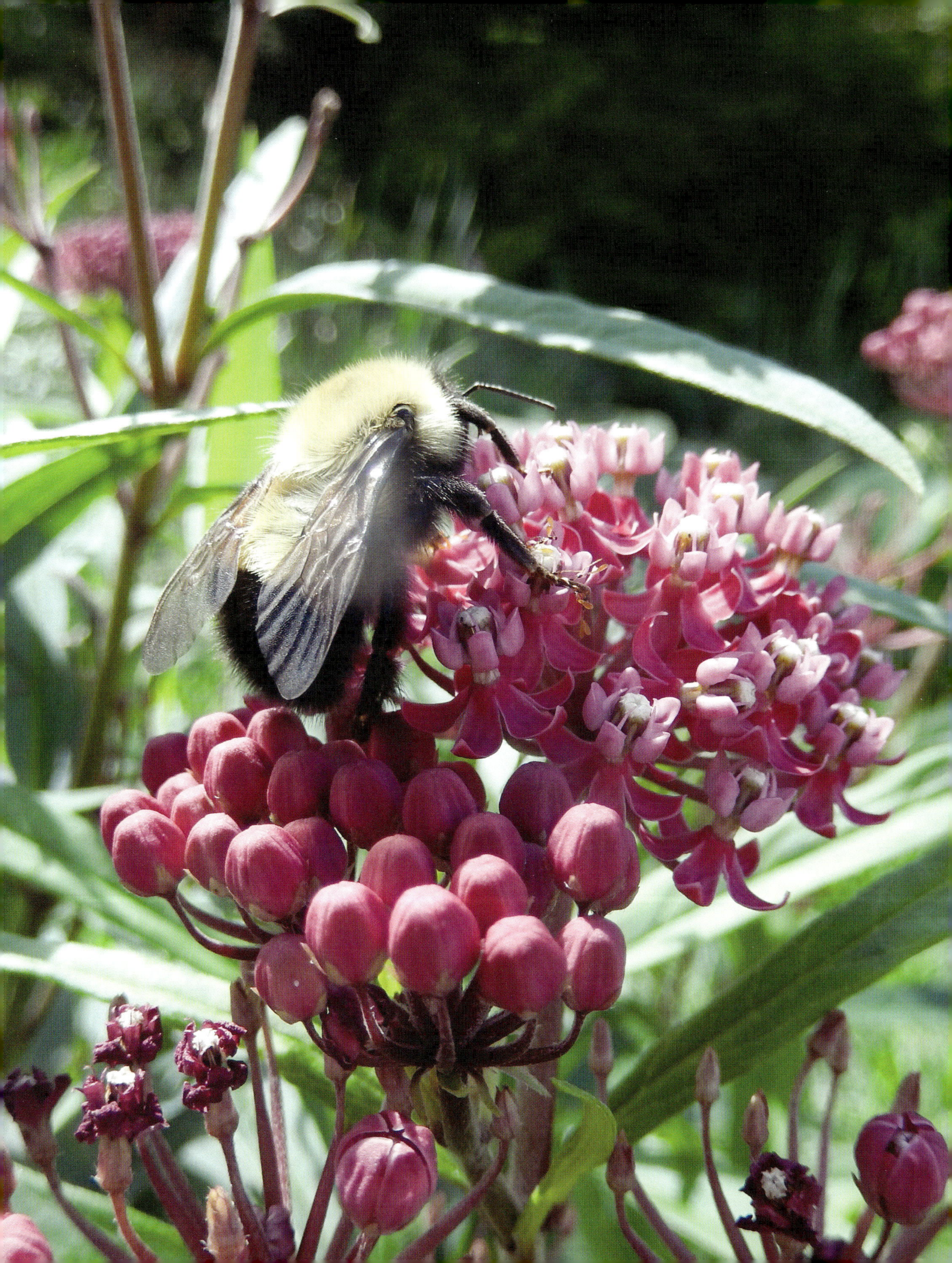

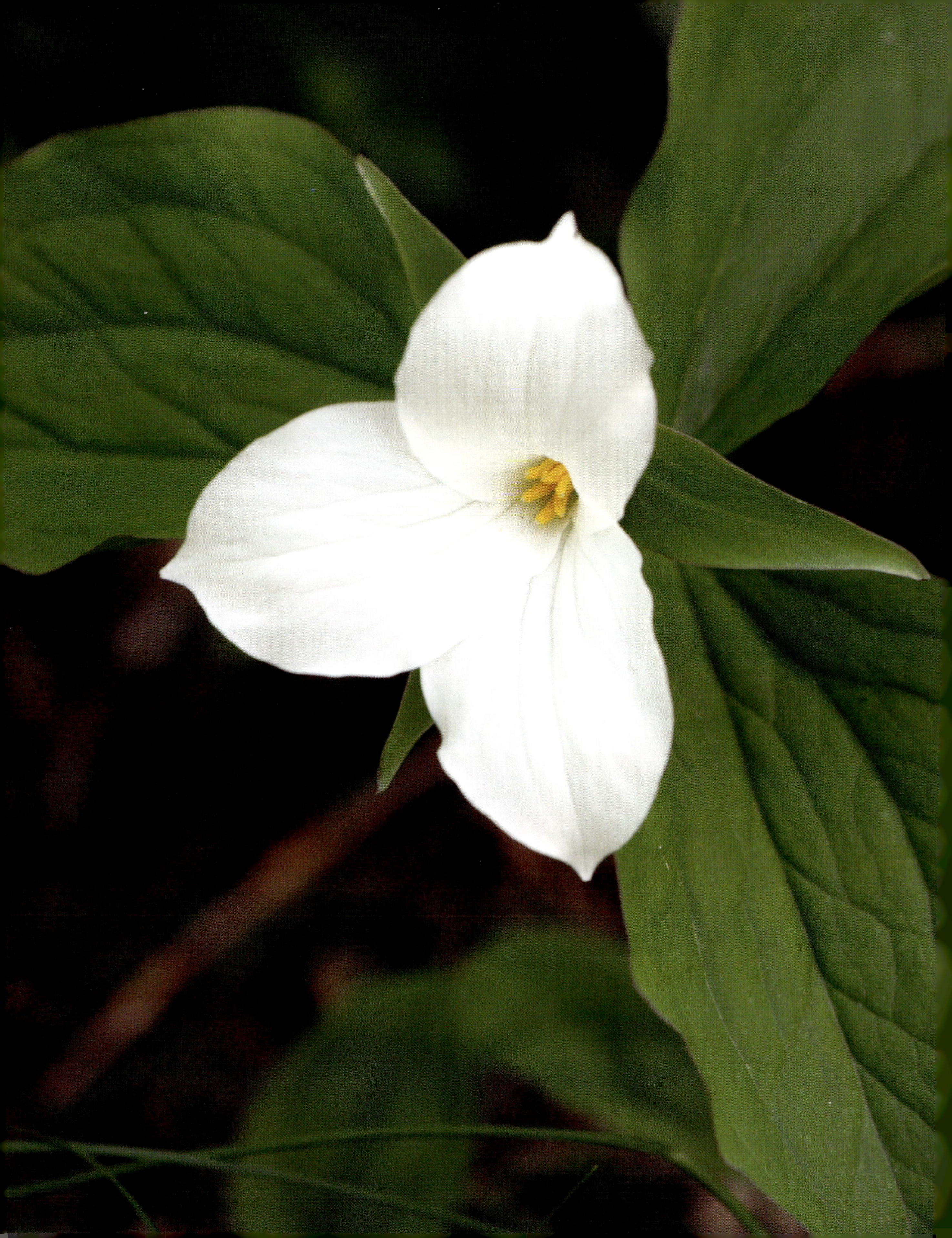

It all began in the kitchen of Bob and Suzanne Lang when she complained that she couldn't find a calendar she liked for the New Year. So they decided to print their own. They used country style pictures and published 800 the first year. By 1982, the calendars pleased the public so much the Langs hired four workers and moved their work to a new building. In 1984 Lang had branched out to calendars, Christmas cards, note cards, and gifts. In 2000, Bob's Boxes, a reusable gift box, was a top-notch seller.

I said, "Oh, that's the Lang Company that prints my kitchen calendar!" I hadn't realized the company was from my own state. Our day of hiking and sight seeing satisfied us immensely, and yet, it humbled me by letting me know I should be more aware of the history of my own state. It just proves there's always more to learn about Wisconsin whether it's geological features, trees, wildlife or interesting history.

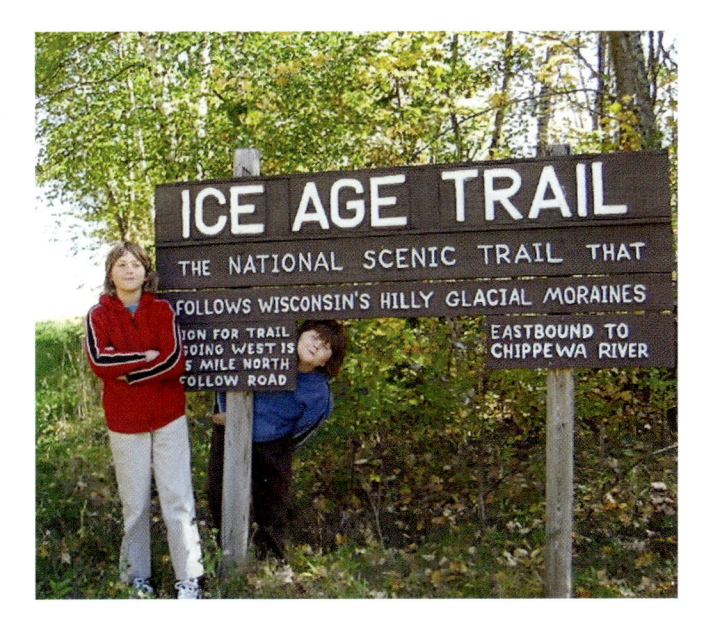

promised to take us back to the very spot on the trail we had left. Soon, we were in a hurry to continue our trek.

To our delight, after we hiked eleven more miles on the Ice Age Trail, the couple met us again and gave us a tour of Delafield, Wisconsin, a very attractive city. Here we learned the Lang Companies, LLC, built homes and restored country style buildings for the city. Theirs is a real success story about a small business that grew.

*Trees increase our love of
home and improve our hearts*
– Increase Lapham

– Sylvia

Spring on the Kettle Moraine

Shades of hepatica, lavender, blue
Petals anemone white and true
Spring beauties blooming for you

Bright yellow trout lilies and marigold
Tiny May apple umbrellas unfold
Lacy green ferns soon to unroll

Fresh spring flowers blooming at once
Clusters of violets in a bunch
Pure white trilliums, can I pick them
Just one?

– Sylvia

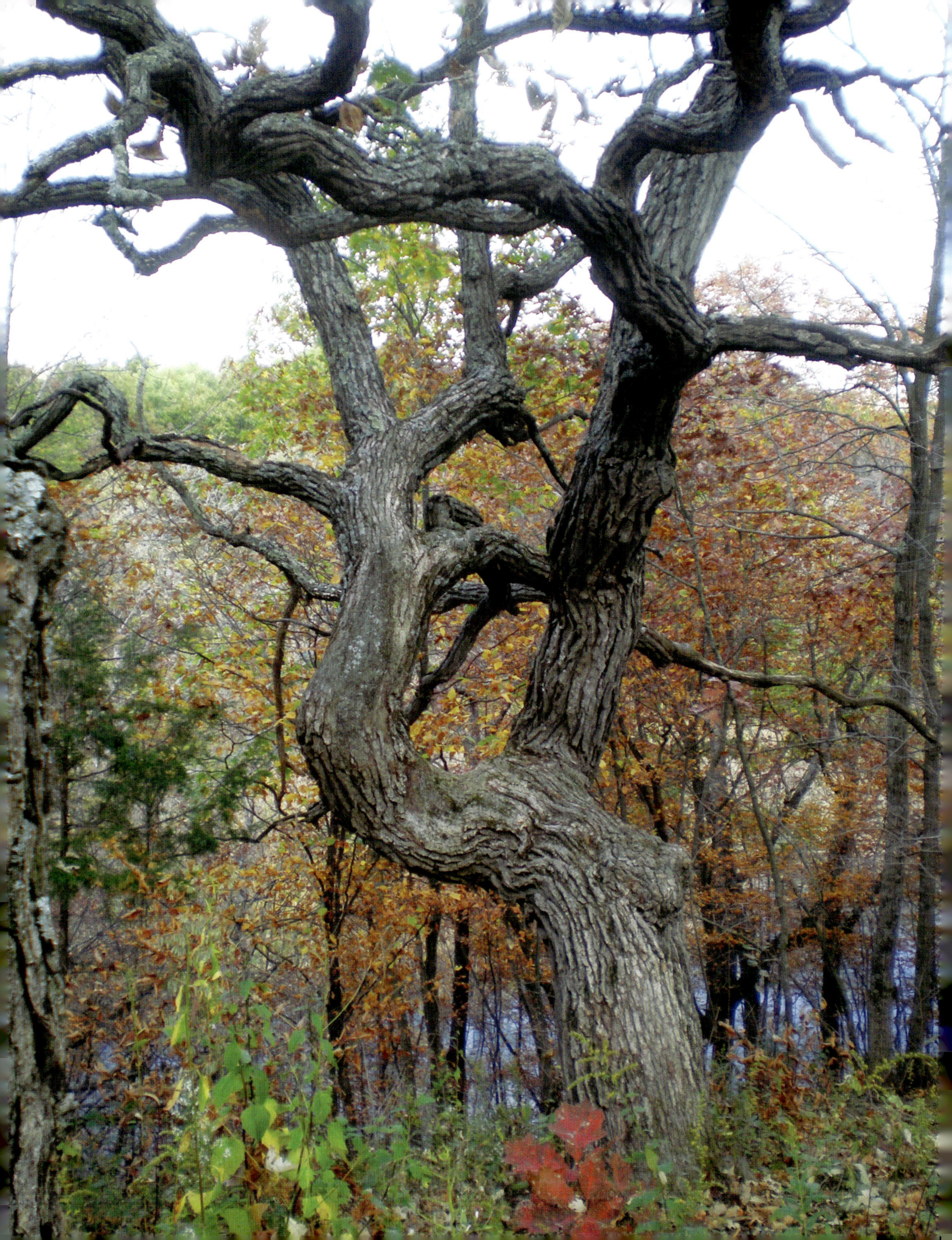

Powder Hill Tower

Southern Holy Hill Segment
Washington County

Walking across grasslands gives a sense of open air and freedom of spirit. It's a walk in nature all the family can enjoy. This area has mixed forest and shrubs especially colorful in the fall. In late summer berries can be seen here and there along the trail. Parts of old stone fences belonging to farmers of the past can be seen in some places.

In the spring the hiker will see wildflowers such as violets, buttercups, and trillium. Birds are plentiful. Squirrels, rabbits, deer and other wildlife frequent this area. Small mammals like chipmunks and mice are fun when they skitter across your walk.

The trail circles the highest glacial kame in Wisconsin and at times the shrine at the top of this hill can be seen from the trail.

A visit to the shrine is an interesting side-trip for those who have extra time.

Pike Lake

Options:

2 miles: From Slinger take Highway 60 west to County Road CC and go south to Pike Lake parking area. Hike to Kettle Moraine Road with a short spur to view Powder Hill Tower.

2 miles: From Hartford take State Highway 83 south to Highway 167. Go east 1.5 miles to County Road K, then south 1 mile to Donegal Road. The trail crosses Donegal Road one-half mile east of K. Hike the trail north to parking near Shannon Road. Trail circles Wisconsin's highest kame (Holy Hill Shrine).

Towers and Spires

My hiking partner and I are almost done
for the day. We began this morning
south of Holy Hill, some thirteen miles
away from here. Climbing up and down
hills, kicking through leaves, dodging rocks
in this ice-scoured landscape, we rested
often, and saw that every bench seemed
strategically placed to view the basilica.

The leaf-covered path, in some places
barely visible, winds around ancient
oak trees as we wade knee-deep
in autumn's glory. The trees
speak their own language
if anyone cares to listen.

We climb Powder Hill Tower,
see Pike Lake and distant towns.
The trees now below our eye level,
stand still, like us, under October's blue.

Turning south, we see the spires
of the basilica, a grand spectacle to some.
For us, the view from the tower is holy:
the sky, the trees, the people below.

– Kris

Climb a Tower for Color

"A tower of Liberty." One high school student used these words to introduce his speech about the United States. The phrase reminds me of the freedom of movement we have in this country and in Wisconsin. Though not the same kind of tower, I've had the liberty to visit a number of these viewing "high spots" on or near the Ice Age Trail.

On a fall day, Kris and I hiked the northern Kettle Moraine and climbed the Parnell Tower near Plymouth, Wisconsin. These towers near and on the Ice Age Trail are fun places to look over the countryside, especially when the fall color bursts upon us. Every time I climb a tower I say, "This is the best one yet!"

The Parnell Tower is built of wood and rises above a four-mile long esker, a rocky deposit formed by water running under a glacier. You ascend the tower by taking 300 steps up. Once you reach the top, you'll look out over beautiful Sheboygan County. Looking to west, one can see the large windmills near Fond du Lac. I had counted over 40 of these large windmills on the ride over to the trail. It pleased and surprised me that we are using that much wind power here in Wisconsin.

Turn to the east and you'll see Sheboygan in the distance. Looking south you see farms with their red barns. It's as if you are looking down from a low flying airplane. Look west and you will see five kames all at the same time. These are cone shaped hills formed from material deposited by the melting glacier. It's neat to be above the kames because you can only see them separately from the trail below.

Other towers to climb near the Ice Age Trail: Timm's Hill, Potawatomi State Park in Door County, Granite Peak in Wausau, and Lapham Peak, near Delafield. These are all great places to view fall color. And don't forget the many trees of the Chequamegon, Grandfather Falls, Baraboo Hills, Dells of the Eau Claire near Wausau, and the colorful trees around the kettle lakes of Chippewa, Barron, and Washburn counties.

How lucky we are to have the liberty and freedom to visit these towers, parks, and bluffs of Wisconsin. So climb a tower to view the color in September and October. The scene will be exciting from those heights. If you can't get to a tower, remember, the parks, lakes and bluffs are there, too. Happy hiking and happy fall color days.

Tower Directions

Parnell Tower, Sheboygan County
Tower is about 9.4 miles from Plymouth
From Plymouth, take State Highway 67 south (goes south then west)
Turn south on County Road A to County Road U
Parking at County Road U Parnell Tower trailhead

Timm's Hill, Price County
From Ogema, take State Highway 86 about 5 miles
Turn south onto County Road C, follow about ¾ mile
Turn east on County Road RR and follow
about ¾ mile to park entrance

Lapham Peak, Waukesha County (Near Delafield)
From I-94 take Exit 285 to County Road C (Kettle Moraine Drive)
Go south 1 mile to Lapham Peak Park main entrance

Powder Hill, Washington County
From Hartford, follow State Highway 60 east 3 miles
to Powder Hill Road and go south .3 miles to parking area

Potawatomi State Park, Door County
From Sturgeon Bay, take State Highway 57/42 southwest
to County Road PD (Park Road)
turn right and go north 2.4 miles to Potawatomi State Park
Parking available in the park and at the tower

Thanks to Dad: I Love Rocks

I have rocks in my head! That's what I say in remembrance of my father and his great love of Wisconsin rocks. Through the years Dad managed to build a rock house, rock garage and a rock milk house. In later years, he would polish agates and set his favorite geodes around on our end tables. I can see him now in his white shirt with the agate tie. He is holding up his favorite black-bubbled rock saying proudly, "This is grape ore."

The rock quarries I walked past near Manitowoc on the Ice Age Trail brought these memories back to me. I felt proud of my great grandfather, who came from Vienna, Austria, and worked in a stone quarry near this city. As the family story goes, he saved another man's life by lifting a boulder off him. It surprised me to see how many quarries are still working in this area. White shale rock is plentiful here, but I learned they sell many different kinds of rock these days.

I'm wishing I'd studied more of our state's geology and could talk with Dad about the rocks. I'd tell how the glacier carved and moved them. I could even tell him that an erratic is a rock carried by the glacier many miles until it sits alone, not matching any rocks in its new location. He'd be proud to know how many rocks I can identify since I've been walking the Ice Age Trail.

I'd talk about the Blue Hills, once a great mountain range, made of 1.6 billion-year-old quartzite and how boulders, frozen and released in the glacier, formed the moraines. In Sauk County moraines blocked both ends of a gorge and created Devil's Lake, our deepest lake. The ice there went out in just a short time and made these rocks some of the most unique in the world. Dells of the St. Croix, Dells of the Eau Claire, red rock granite of central, and the white shale in eastern Wisconsin are all most interesting. I'd tell Dad about the large square rocks of Waupaca County that surprised us. And I'm looking forward to a trail hike near Baraboo that has that large Gibraltar Rock.

Thanks to that dad of mine with his interest in rocks, his enthusiasm spread to our family and others. Dads, take a cue from mine, and take your children to see some rocks on the trails and in the state parks of Wisconsin. Rocks can make good viewing and good memories.

– Sylvia

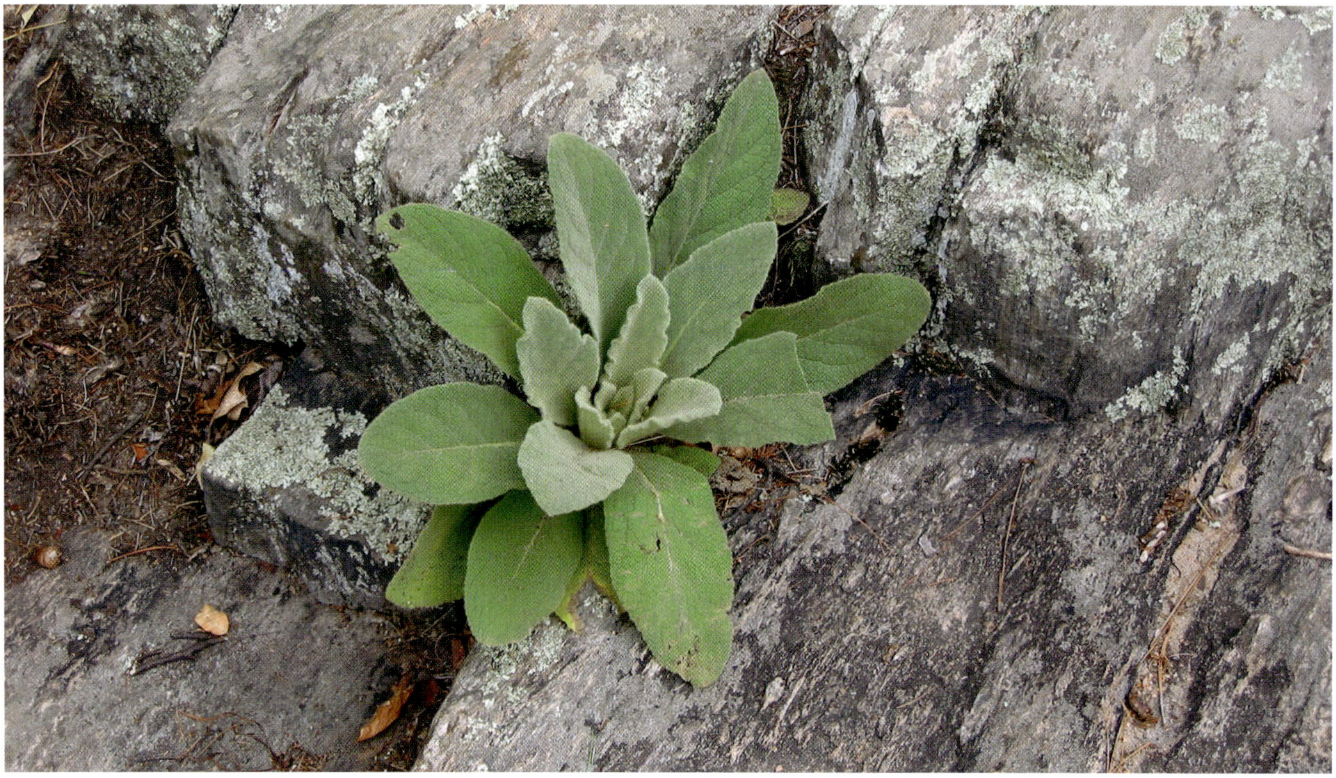

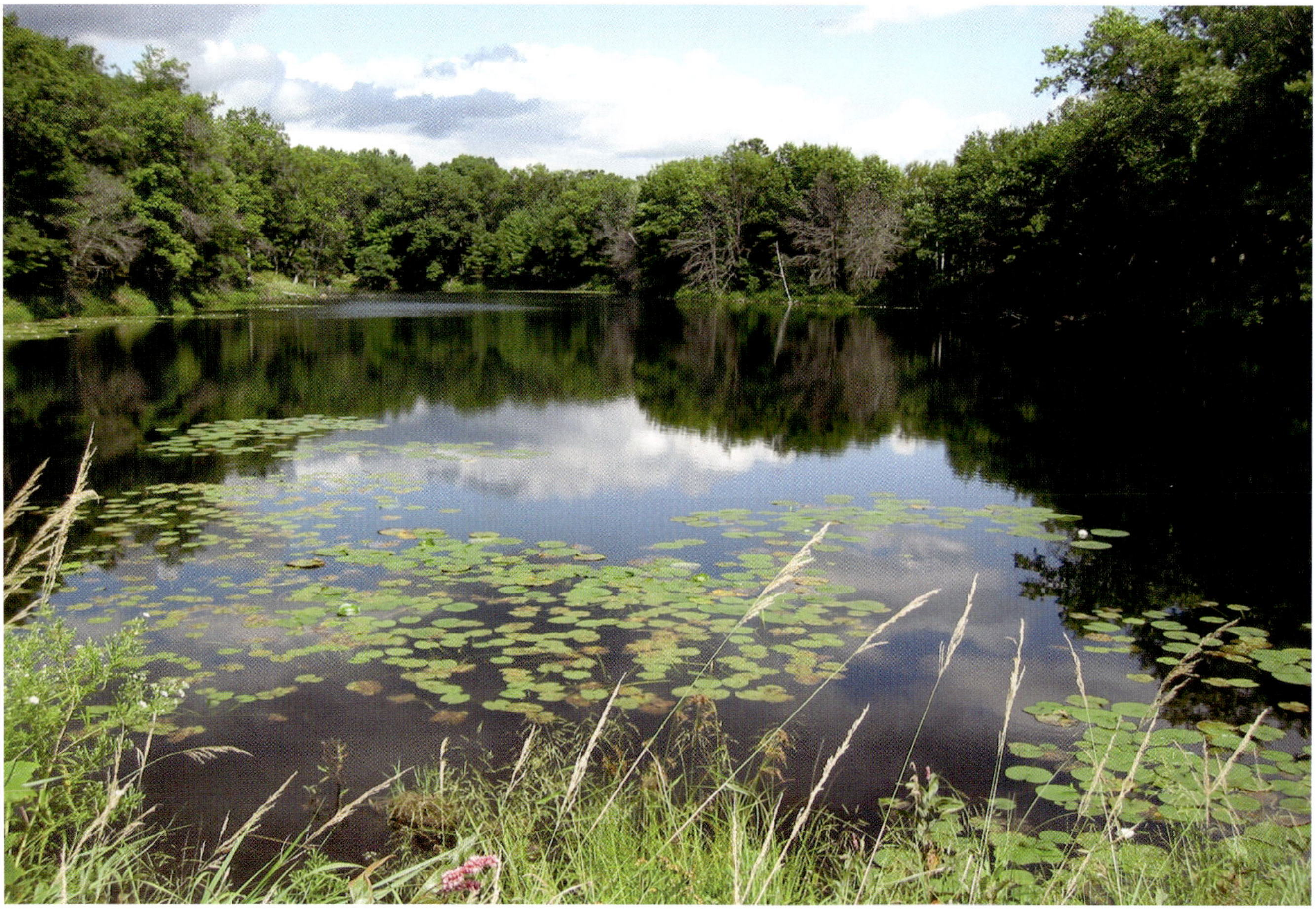

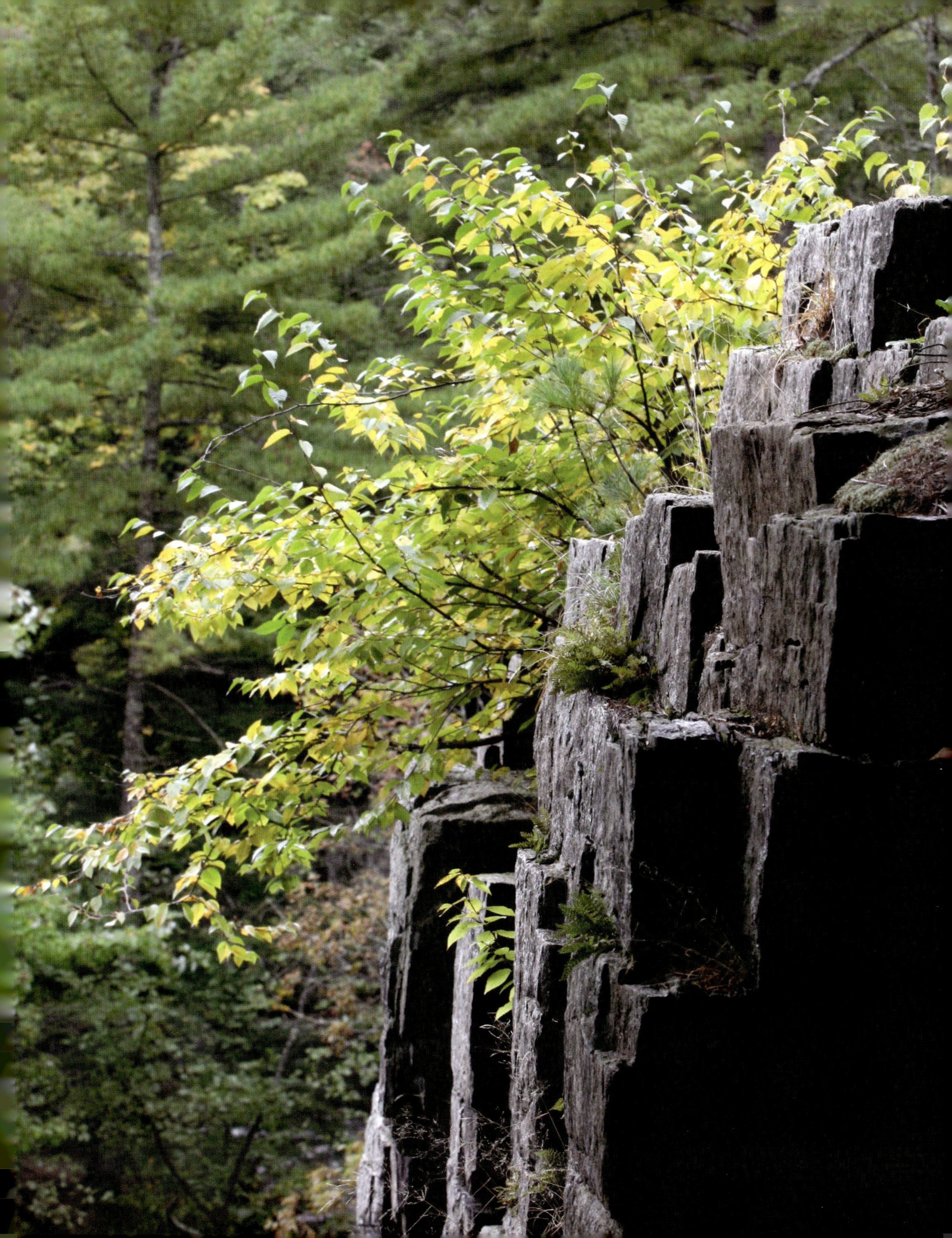

Manitowoc

rusty town
of sailors
shipbuilders
and the kyrie
of seagulls

– Kris

The Ice Age Trail
On and Near Rustic Roads

In Kewaunee County you will see open farmland and fields that border Lake Michigan in many places. Some farm fields end right at water's edge, a different topography than we see on the farms in mid-state Wisconsin. There are black barns trimmed in white instead of traditional red. Often fog "creeps in on little cat feet" like the Sandburg poem. It's an excellent hike for photos. Gulls and cranes are plentiful. On sunny days red-winged blackbirds and even some bluebirds may fly overhead.

At Point Beach Segment, Manitowoc County, you will walk along the beach for two miles on the shores of Lake Michigan. An Ice Age Trail map should be used for this, as it may be easy to miss the yellow blaze signs, especially when the trail continues on into a wooded area.

Point Beach State Forest offers camping, hiking, and picnic area and more. Not far from the Ice Age parking area there is a trail to Rawley Point Lighthouse, a tall octagonal tower, the only one of its kind on the Great lakes. Red pine trees, ancient beach ridges, wetlands, and sand dunes are some features of this section.

In Waupaca County Rustic Road 57 on South Foley Road, you can see where several glacial advances occurred. The narrow moraines here that were deposited thousands of years ago are not continuous because of the unique way the glaciers melted. The hiker will see many drumlins (long narrow hills of glacial drift) and rigid hills. The trail passes a gigantic erratic boulder, one of the trail's largest rocks. Erratics are boulders carried long distances by the glaciers and deposited when the glacier melted.

Options:

3.5 miles: Kewanee County. An interesting day hike. Parking at Bruemmer County Park, on County Road C, on the Kewaunee River west of Kewaunee. Hike from there to Father Marquette Memorial Park on Lake Michigan in Kewaunee.

7 miles: Begin at Bruemmer County Park west of Kewaunee and continue through Kewaunee on Lakeshore Drive north to 1st Road

4.5 miles: Two Rivers, Manitowoc County. Parking at Rawley Point Lighthouse off County Road O (Sandy Bay Road) four miles north of Two Rivers. Hike to Park Road along Lake Michigan Point Beach Segment.

6.5 miles: Waupaca County. From parking at Skunk and Foster Lake on North Foley Drive, walk south to Cobb Town. For longer 8-mile hike continue on Townline Road to parking on Highway 54. Watch for route changes on this section.

Road Walk on the IAT
Variety, Spice for a Walk

Hiking along on the Ice Age Trail road connector near Westfield, I felt my heart skip a few beats. Just ahead, I saw a wild pig. It was standing still and seemed to be glaring at me. I walked closer. Whew! It's just a lawn ornament! That was a relief and it cheered me to realize it was just another in the huge variety of lawn decorations Wisconsinites love to display.

It's fun, while walking the road connectors on the Ice Age Trail, to notice which ornaments are most popular in an area. I've taken an unofficial tally. My daughter wrote down a list and every time we saw one, we made a mark. So far, the three most prominent lawn ornaments are the wishing well, deer, and windmills.

The traditions behind the wishing well are many. In ancient times water itself was considered holy and certain wells were considered prophetic. For example, St. Helen's Well at Staffordshire, England, dried up just before a calamity. Tradition says this well dried up before the execution of Charles I, even in a wet season. Coins dropped in wishing wells for healing can be traced back to the Greeks and Romans.

We have enough wind here in Wisconsin for the many windmills that spin in many shapes and colors. They are decorative and useful, too. Some people use them to disguise the pipes coming from their holding tanks. Windmills are often accompanied by the Dutch boy and Dutch girl, reminding us of the Netherlands.

I did not research anything about the many deer statues we saw in yards along the way. I just think I know how honored deer are in Wisconsin. My daughter always laughed and said, "Mother, if we become a future generation's archeological dig, they will think we worshiped deer!" And according to my grandfather, the beautiful white tail, big brown eyes and graceful body make the deer much better looking than people.

Another ornament high on our list is the gazing ball of blue, green and deep red. These would make my husband shake his head, wondering why anyone would want them, but I liked the reflections they made for my photographs. Gazing balls called kugels (kugel means ball in Germany) were placed at the gate in the front yard so people sitting on porches could see who was coming and quickly close the door or go to prepare a cup of tea.

I saw many more unique ornaments like the wheelbarrow filled with flowers spilling out, shrines, wagon wheels, mushrooms and even Packers on a swing. It made me think there's at least one good thing about having a late spring. It gives us time to dust off, unwrap or repaint our decorations. Every year our neighbor takes the blanket off his dog statue. His Lassie looks new and clean, but I often have to repaint my wooden daisy that says, "Welcome." Then I know, "Spring has sprung!"

– Sylvia

Ice Age Trail, Maplewood

Once-busy farming town lies nearly fallow,
trains long silent, elevators empty.

Like a long-married couple,
two deer-bodied cranes
take an afternoon stroll.

Geese waddle along the trail,
gossiping, barely turning
slender necks to glance,
pop-eyed, at intruders.

A hawk screes and circles,
embroiders a patch of blue.

– Kris

Sturgeon Bay Segment – Eastern Terminus
Door County

On the shore of Sawyer Harbor, where the waters of Sturgeon Bay meet Green Bay, a 75-foot observation tower marks the eastern terminus of the Ice Age Trail, at the north end of Potawatomi State Park. As this is a state park, visitors must have either a state park sticker for their cars or a daily admission fee is charged. The park contains a campground, picnic areas, restrooms, and water.

Watch carefully for the yellow blazes that mark the Ice Age Trail, as the park also contains Tower Trail and Hemlock Trail. From the tower, the Ice Age Trail goes through woods before descending to the shoreline of Sturgeon Bay. The trail meanders through the park, climbing uphill through wooded areas and again descends back to the shoreline.

At the south end of the park, the trail continues on Duluth Avenue, following a well-marked route through the streets of Sturgeon Bay. On the south side of Sturgeon Bay, the trail joins Ahnapee State Trail, a converted railroad track that was converted into a multi-use recreational trail.

Directions:

To reach the eastern terminus of the Ice Age Trail, take State Highway 57/42 southwest of Sturgeon Bay to County Highway PD (Park Road). Turning right, go north 2.4 miles to Potawatomi State Park. The observation tower is on the north edge of the park, approximately 3.5 miles from Highway PD.

Parking:

Parking is available at the observation tower and throughout the park.

Options:

The distance from the north end of Potawatomi State Park to the south end is approximately two miles. A pleasant day trip allows ample time for exploring the other trails in the park and for climbing the tower.

Walking through Sturgeon Bay adds another 3.5 miles. The Ahnapee State Trail continues for over 15 miles, almost to Algoma, although not all portions of it are considered part of the Ice Age Trail due to motorized use.

Meeting Jason Dorgan
A Door County Ice Age Trail Adventure

My trail companions had become fascinated with the journey of Jason Dorgan, a Madison area runner who decided to run the entire Ice Age Trail in a two-week period in April 2007. Assisted by ground support, Jason updated his progress daily on a blog. He stayed in motels each night, soaking his legs in an ice cube filled bathtub after each day's run. Upon seeing that Jason planned to stay overnight in Gilman, Gene emailed to let him know that Gilman was too small to contain any motels and made recommendations for a motel in nearby Thorp.

Sylvia and Gene made a point of meeting Jason where his run crossed a road near their home, and Gene even agreed to wash Jason's clothes for him. As they were lightweight runners' togs, Gene noted, "There was nothing to them."

After meeting Jason they were even more interested in his adventure and continued to follow his progress. They knew that Jason was on track to complete his journey at Potawatomi State Park on May 6, 2007. They decided meet him at the park as he completed his run and invited me to join them.

After meeting several of Jason's friends and fellow running club members at the observation tower, we walked about a quarter mile on the trail to greet him and cheer for him as he came through. His friends ran the final leg with him while we chose our favorite pace: walking. Making an updated report via his cellphone as he approached the observation tower, Jason admitted that the end felt a bit anti-climactic. He completed his run at 12:34 p.m. on 5/6/7.

After meeting Jason and congratulating him with a bottle of wine from a local winery, we stayed in the park to walk. A glorious spring day with trillium in bloom, it felt wonderful to be outside. After walking so many isolated areas, it felt odd for us to be in a state park that is obviously well loved, and well attended, with paths that are well used and easy to see. Even though the paths were easy to follow, it was a bit challenging, as other trails also run throughout the park. We were careful to check the trail signs at all intersections.

Although we saw many other families and couples enjoying the park that day (a Sunday afternoon), we were still able to find quiet and solitude, especially by the water. We savored the variety of sights, from high on the observation tower to walking in the woods to checking for boats passing by as we walked along the water. We also learned about the rock upon which we stood: a dolomite bluff that is part of the Niagara Escarpment.

We continued walking through Sturgeon Bay, a picturesque city with bridges and boats. If you visit, be sure to look for a quaint diner and order a piece of cherry pie (made with Door County cherries, of course!) and topped with a generous scoop of cinnamon ice cream.

– Kris

One More Tower

What shall I wear? Do I have my backpack, camera and flashlight? Hmm, should I take moleskin in case of a blister or spray for bugs? Maybe I should take a warmer coat, but if I get hiking, this lighter one will do. Well, you can't take the kitchen sink, for heavens sake! After all, it's only a one-day hike on the Ice Age Trail.

It was a great October bright-blue-sky day so we packed pretty light. Friend Kris and I set out eagerly on our 12 mile trek to cover the two segments of trail I had left: Holy Hill and Pike Lake. My dream of becoming a "thousand-miler" was finally in sight.

The Holy Hill segment of the Ice Age trail runs very near the shrine. The steeples can be seen for miles as the hiker goes up and down hills. Our plan had been to walk south to Holy Hill but changed because we thought, "Hike those hills first."

The largest kame in southern Wisconsin is Holy Hill. "Like the sands of an hour glass" is a good way to describe how a cone-shaped hill called a kame is formed. As the glacier began to melt, holes in the ice allowed materials to sift through like sand in an hourglass. Time passed. The ice went out around this build-up and left

ICE AGE TRAIL
HOLY HILL SEGMENT

A PUBLIC FOOT TRAIL ACROSS PRIVATE
LANDS FOR HIKERS – NO VEHICLES OR HORSES
NO CAMPING OR FIRES. PLEASE
RESPECT THE LAND YOU TRAVEL THROUGH

ICE AGE
NATIONAL SCENIC TRAIL

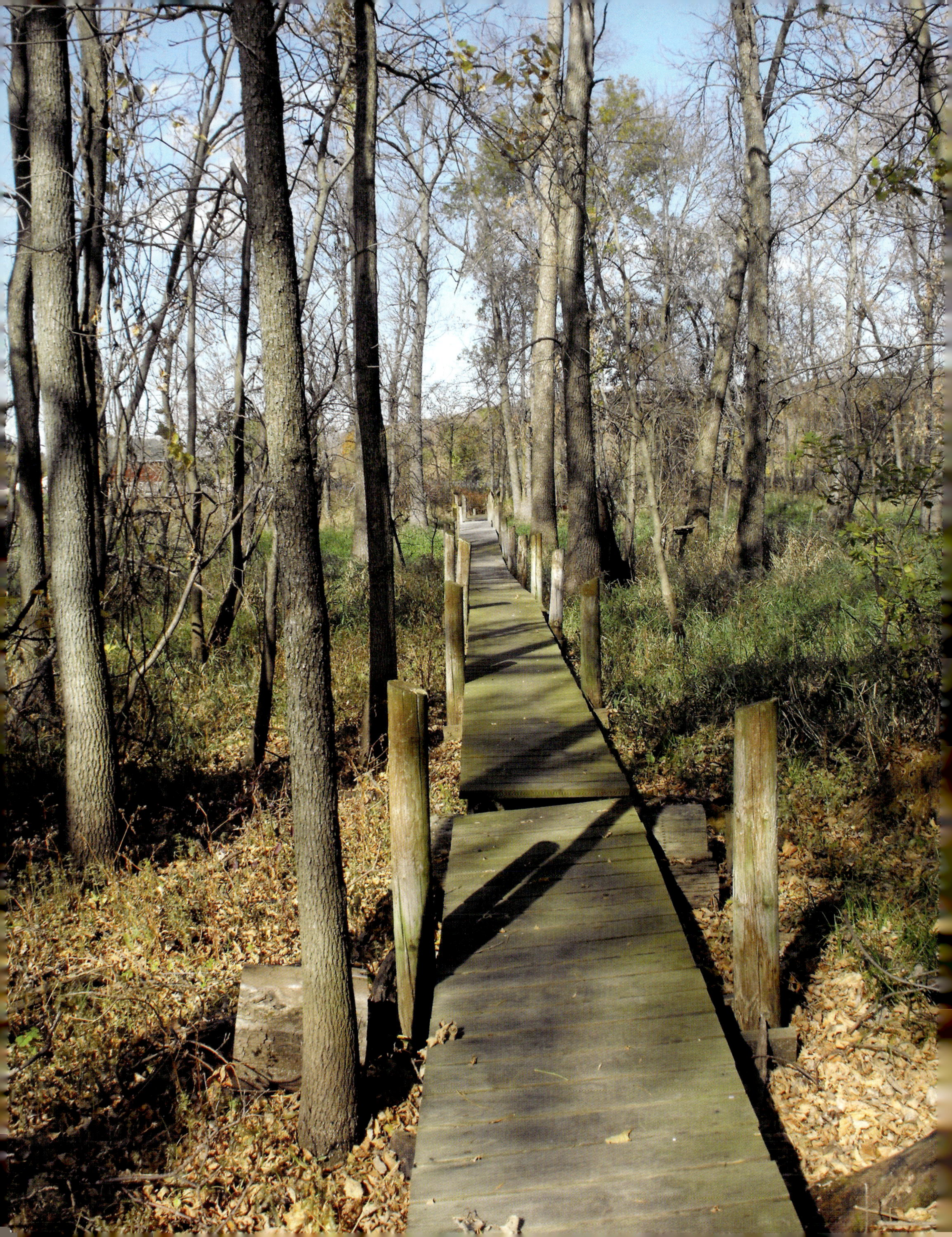

behind the triangular shaped hill. Thanks to the glacier we have this awesome hill that almost took our breath away.

At the top, Holy Hill is 1,350 feet above sea level, and you can see the Milwaukee skyline some thirty miles away. Once known as Government Hill, it was purchased by a priest, a log chapel built, and later became a basilica and a National Registered Historic Place. Today, visitors can climb the 178 steps to the tower and look over the countryside.

After Holy Hill, we swished along in the fallen leaves glad to see some late fall color while squirrels gathered acorns from the many large oaks along the trail. An Aldo Leopold bench placed there by a Scout group was the perfect place to sit and eat lunch. Just then, hundreds of blackbirds came flocking up above our heads. I was marveling how they fly without crashing each other when one dropped a little present on the sleeve of my jacket. At least it didn't hit my sandwich!

Because I hadn't read the guidebook carefully, I had another pleasant surprise three hours later while hiking the Pike Lake segment. The sign said take a side trip to another tower ahead. Imagine, another tower! Powder Hill Tower is a wooden tower built on the second highest kame on the southern Kettle Moraine. It was amazing how far we could see from this tower: two lakes, several towns and cities, windmills, Holy Hill's steeples, and lots of country. This was the best tower yet! My goal was clearly in sight.

We climbed down and continued hiking the last quarter mile of trail. In a minute, an 83 year old man came jogging along beside us. He said he was very thankful for the trail because otherwise he would just be home watching TV. He had run a marathon the week before at Mt. Morris, Wisconsin. He uses this part of the Ice Age trail for good practice.

Tears came to my eyes as I reached this finish line. I wiped them away and the runner kindly took our picture next to the trail sign. If only my husband Gene and daughter Marie could be welcoming me. I know they would be so proud! I couldn't believe it. By the time I got home, I had a dozen messages on Facebook. Someone left champagne and roses waiting on my doorstep. Oh my, I'm famous! All 1,099 miles completed. I'm a thousand-miler at last!

– Sylvia

Thanks, Coach

(October 21, 2011)
He played on a softball team while his wife
chased their toddlers around the park.
He followed the Thorp Cardinals in every season,
driving across the state when the girls made the playoffs.
After hip replacements he gave up walking,
became the driver when his wife walked the Ice Age Trail
He read the maps, planned each day's adventures,
plotted road connectors before they were added to the atlas,
drove ahead while his wife walked,
recruiting friends and family to join in their trail trips.

He listened to the Brewers game all afternoon
while we walked along the canal through Portage.
Waited in the car "for my walkers" he'd say,
when farmers and cops stopped to ask if he was ok.
"I'll give you seven miles today," he'd tell us
at the end of our day's walk, kept a tally of totals for all.
A heart attack, dialysis, he still kept going,
coaching "his walkers" up to his last days.
A bittersweet day-- today, Sylvia finished in honor of
his memory, and I was there with her. "Thanks, coach,"
you got me started on this walk. Now I, too,
vow to finish the Ice Age Trail in your memory.

– Kris

Ice Age National Scenic Trail

Acknowledgments

To my husband, Gene, and daughter, Marie, for their support during the many walks we enjoyed outdoors in nature.

To New Auburn Interpretive Center for my first Ice Age Trail hike.

To Don and Jan Erickson, of Superior Lobe, for introducing me to the trail and its beauty.

Also to family members and friends who shared walks with me, especially Kris Rued-Clark, who walked over 350 miles with me, taking photos, learning about nature in Wisconsin, and enjoying the unique features left by glaciers of the past.

– Sylvia

With gratitude to Sylvia for introducing me to the Ice Age Trail and being my trail-walking buddy.

With loving thoughts in memory of Gene Oberle, who relished being our driver and coach.

In appreciation for the Ice Age Trail Alliance and all those volunteers who have built the trail and maintain the trail.

With many thanks for the landowners who graciously allow segments of the trail to cross their property.

With enthusiastic anticipation for all those who have yet to discover the Ice Age Trail. May you love it as much as we do.

Thanks to thousand-miler Dianne Genz who helped shape our vision for this book.

Special thanks to Cody Popp for designing our book and for Rodger Beyer and the helpful team at Worzalla Publishing for bringing our project to fruition.

– Kris

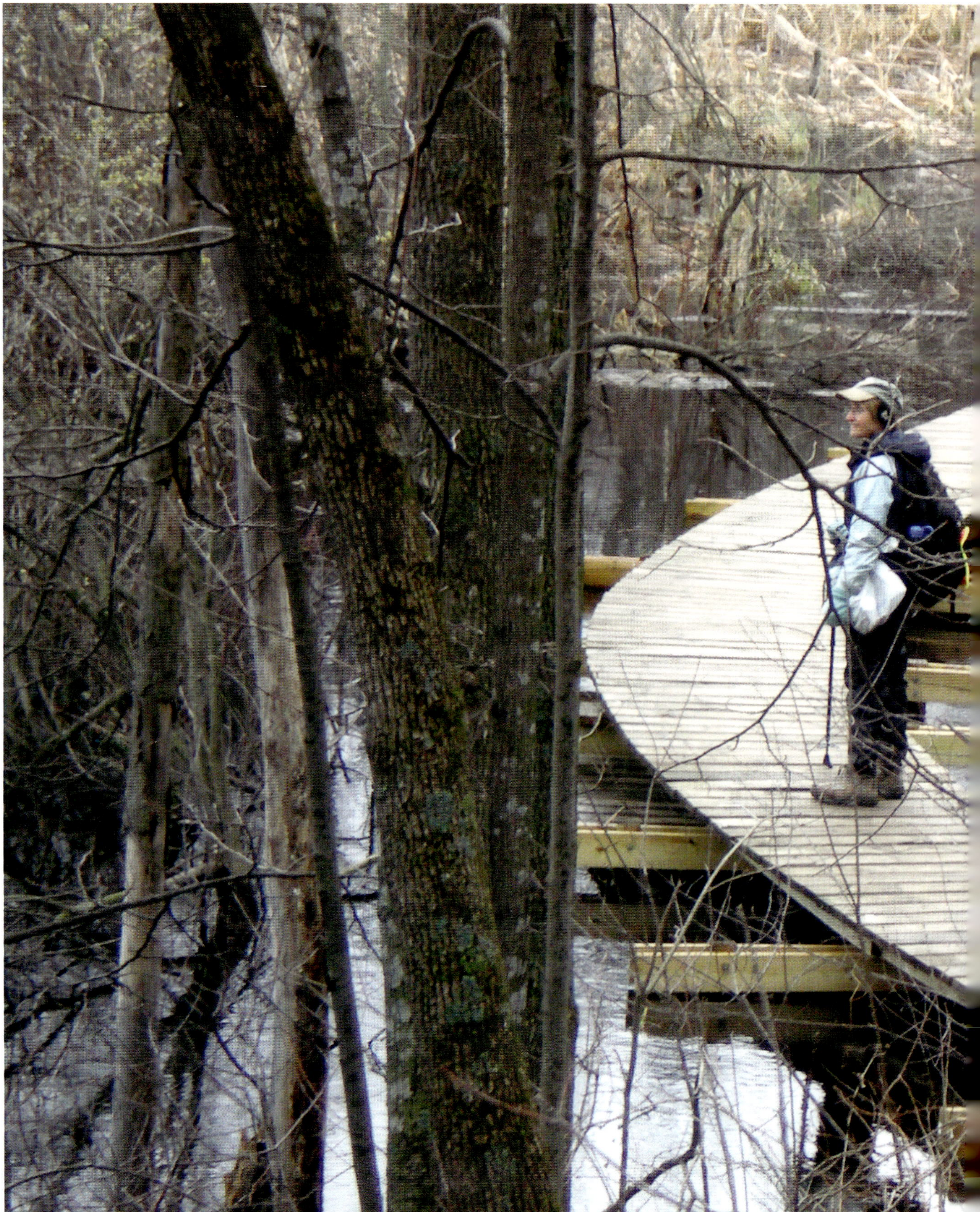

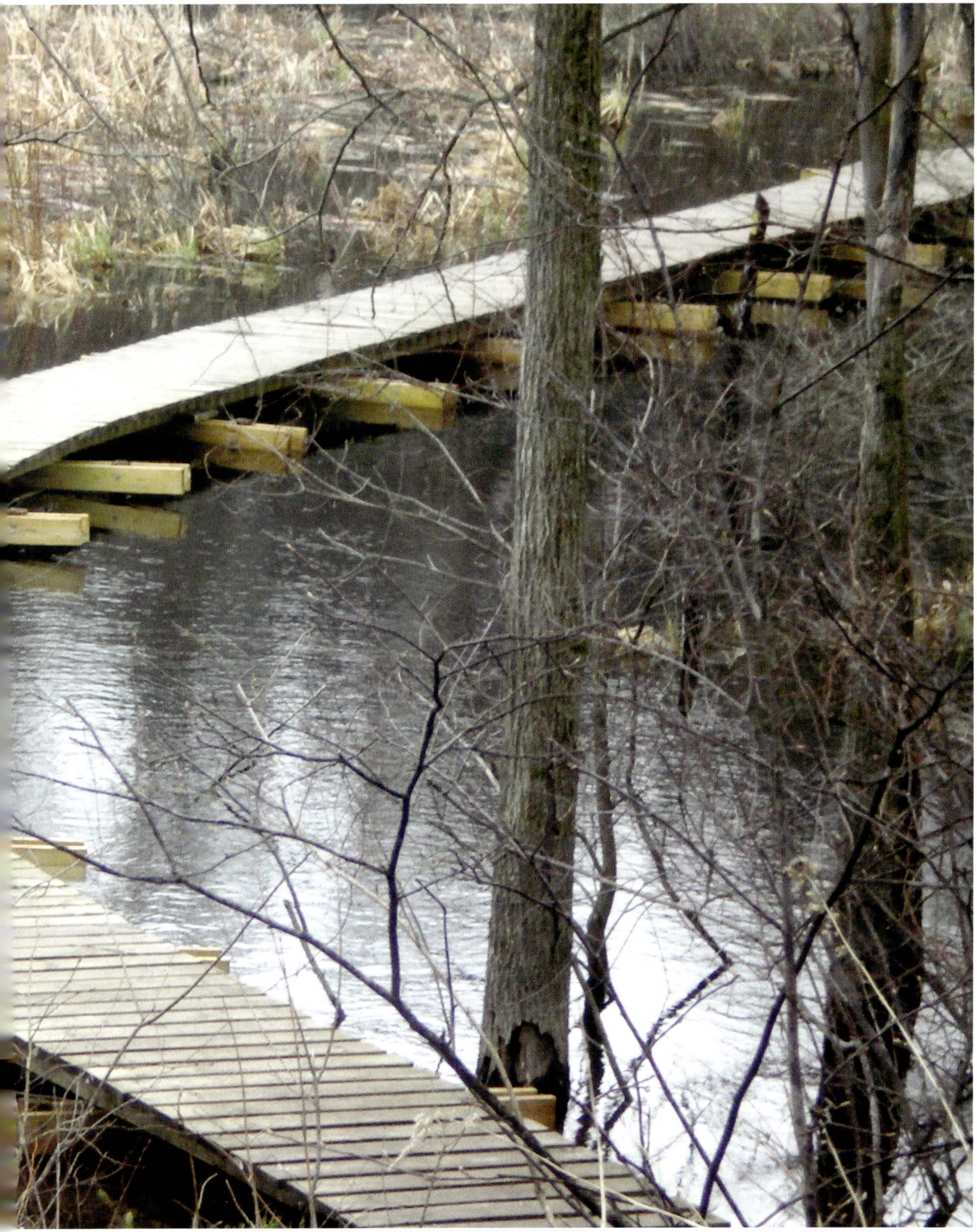

Sylvia Oberle

Kristine Rued-Clark

About the Authors

Sylvia Oberle is a Thorp, Wisconsin, teacher, active in environmental studies, with an interest in conservation, photography, and writing. Her nonfiction has been published in Country Woman, Good Old Days, NEA Magazine, and Mammoth Tales. Her essay on Health Care in Wisconsin earned an honorable mention by Wisconsin Regional Writers.

Sylvia first learned about the Ice Age Trail when she attended the dedication of the new Chippewa Moraine Interpretive Center in 1993. The facility is located near New Auburn. Groups of people, including Congressman Dave Obey, walked two-mile and five-mile segments before the ceremony. Her experience that day piqued her interest and it wasn't long before she wanted to hike the entire length of it. She persisted in her goal, finishing the thousand miles in honor of her husband Gene and daughter Marie.

Sylvia believes family health improves when time is spent taking walks in nature.

It is her wish that Ice Age Trail short-walks or day-hikes will be an adventure for others.

Kris Rued-Clark began walking the Ice Age Trail in 2005. She planned to write an article about Sylvia Oberle and her experiences on the Ice Age Trail, and Sylvia said, "If you're going to write about the Ice Age Trail, you really need to experience it first." That first walk, on the Eau Claire Dells segment, was enough to get Kris hooked on the trail, and she offered to walk with Sylvia whenever time permitted. She felt honored to be the one walking along when Sylvia reached her goal of completing the trail. As of this writing, Kris has completed 400 miles of the Ice Age Trail and intends to become a thousand-miler like Sylvia. An avowed tree hugger and rock lover, Kris lives near Arpin, Wisconsin, almost the exact geographic center of the state, with her husband, Steve, and their five spoiled cats. Kris is a freelance writer and editor, and this is her first book.

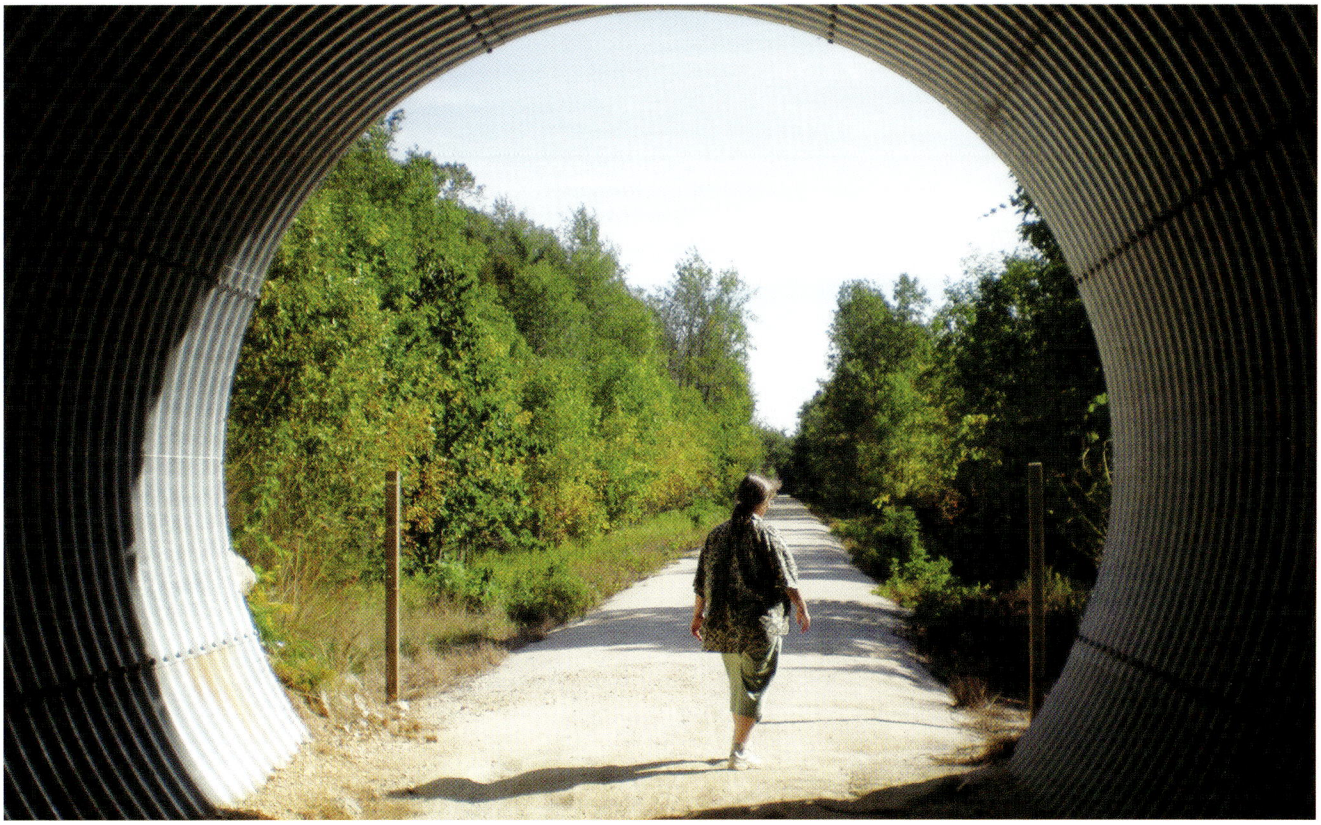

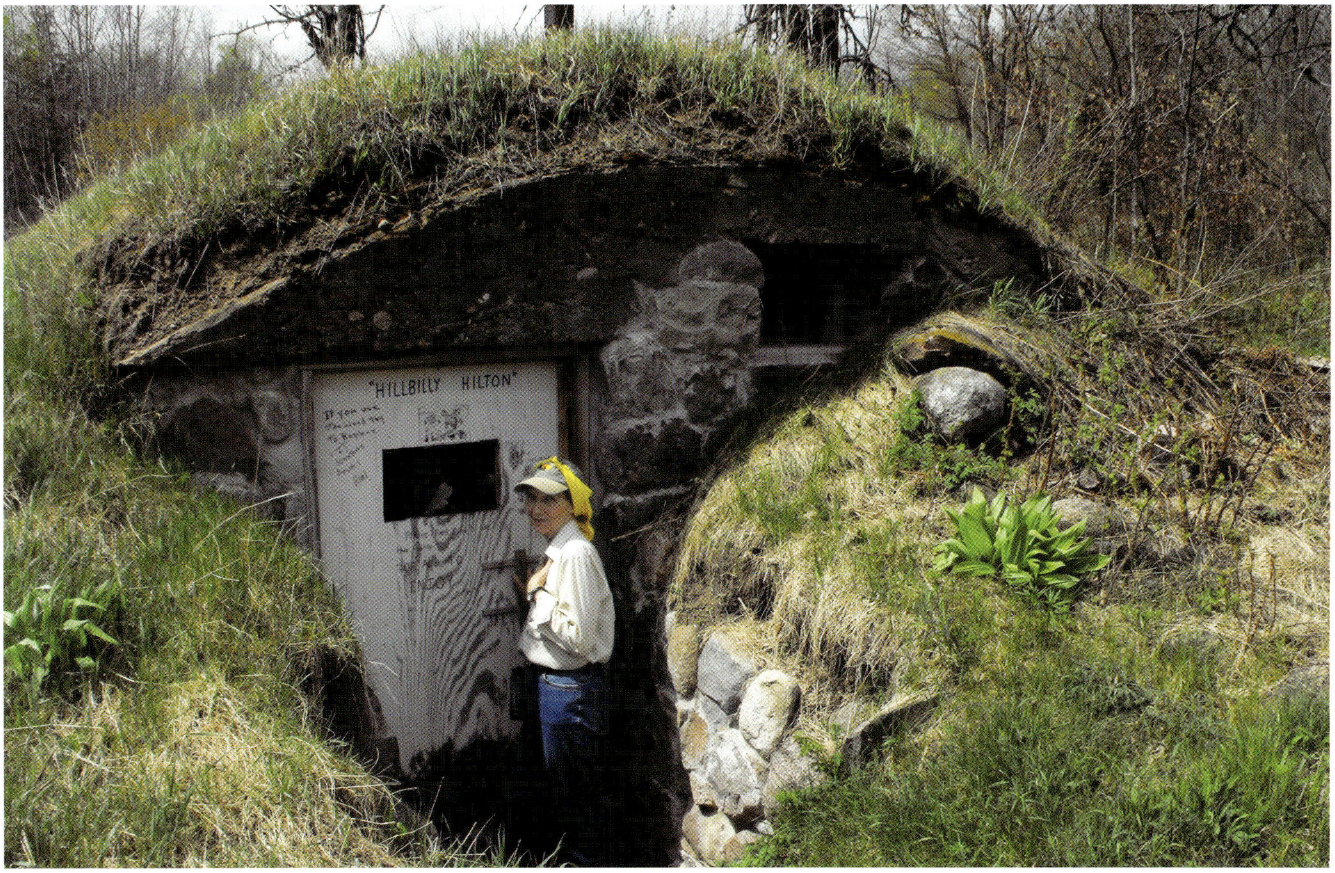
"HILLBILLY HILTON"

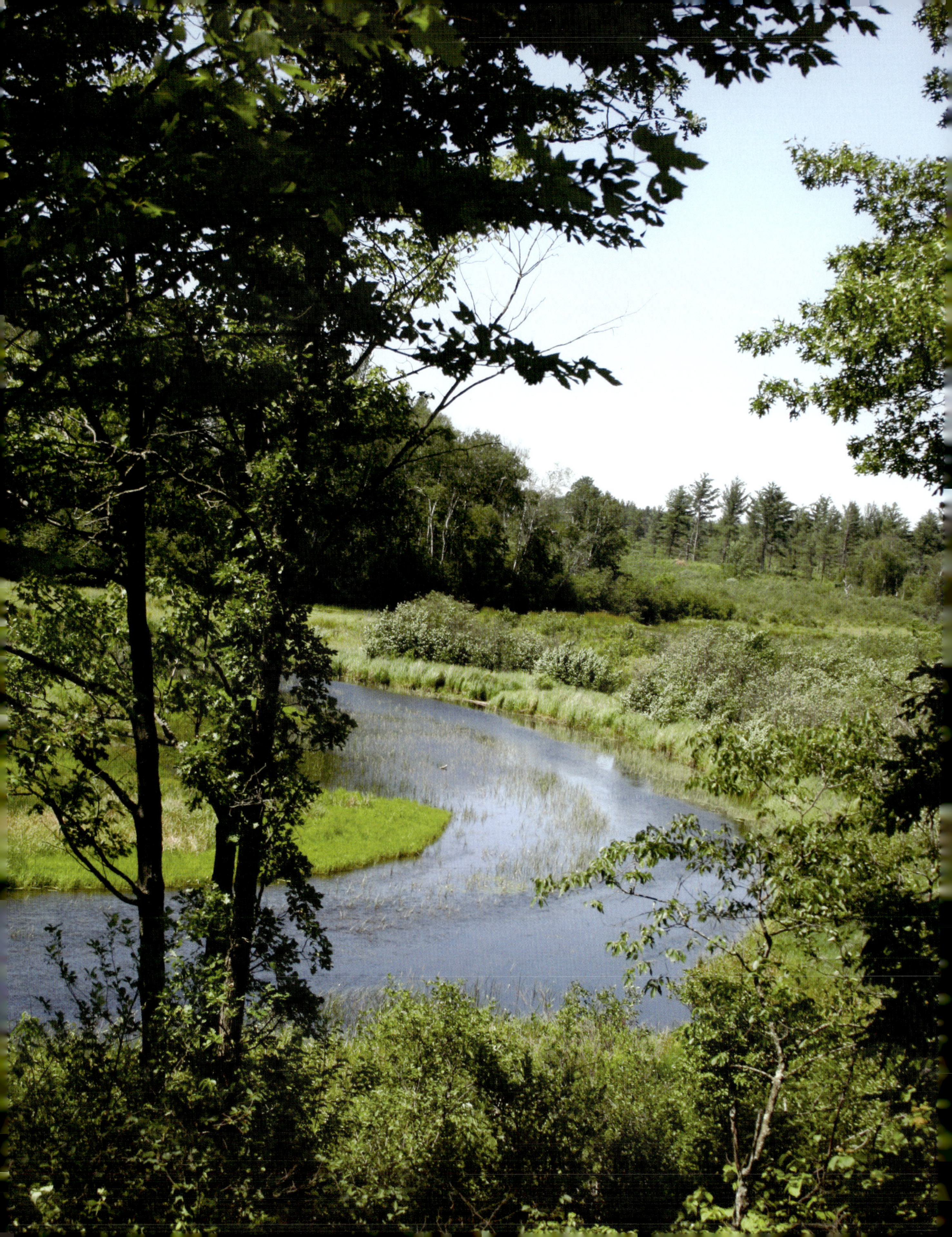

Wanderer's Haiku

to find your way out
of a forest you're lost in
look for lighter sky

— Kris

For Gene

In the perfume of new-mown hay,
    remember me.
When a leaf dances on a maple tree
and a breeze whispers in the forest,
    feel my touch.
In the rush of snow-fed rivers,
    hear my chuckle.
When a cardinal sings in winter's hush,
    know that I look over you still.
In the promise of the rainbow,
    I, too, soar free.

— Kris

All photographs by Sylvia Oberle except where indicated
* denotes photographs by Kristine Rued-Clark

Front Cover: *Dunes Segment, Manitowoc County

Back Cover: *Milwaukee River Segment, Fond du Lac County

Title Page: City of Two Rivers Segment, Manitowoc County

p. 6, Verona Segment, Dane County

p. 7, Sylvia Oberle's photograph of David R. Obey, taken at the Ice Age Interpretive Center, New Auburn, Chippewa County, first appeared on the jacket of his book, Raising Hell for Justice, published by The University of Wisconsin Press, © 2007, and is reprinted here with permission

p. 8, hepatica, North Kettle Moraine Forest near Glenbeulah, Sheboygan County

p. 9, *trail sign, Lumber Camp Segment, Langlade County

p. 10, clockwise from upper left, *Wood Lake Segment, Taylor County; *Kelly Creek, Wau-Mo Segment, Lincoln County; IAT Alliance convention, 2012

p. 12 trunk fungi, Tuscobia Trail, Barron County

p. 13, pitcher plant on floating bog, Old Railroad Segment, Langlade County

p. 14, *Townline Lake, Highland Lakes Western Segment, Langlade County

P. 15 Fritillary butterfly

p. 16 clockwise from upper left, autumn trees, Kettle Lake, New Auburn Segment, Chippewa County; fungi, Grandfather Falls Segment, Lincoln County; trail sign, Portage Canal Segment, Columbia County

p. 17 Wood Lake Segment, Taylor County

p. 18, Jerry Lake Segment, Taylor County

p. 19, black-eyed Susan, road walk

pp. 21-23, St. Croix Falls Segment, Western Terminus of the Ice Age Trail, Polk County

p. 24, bears, photos by Rick Koziel

p. 27, left, New Wood Segment, Lincoln County; right, Wood Lake Segment, Taylor County

p. 28, wetland, John Muir Park, Marquette County

P. 29, Taylor County

p. 31, McKenzie Creek Segment, Polk County

p. 32, *top photo, Pine Lake Segment, Polk County

p. 32, bottom photo and pp. 33-34, Pine Lake and Straight River Segments, Polk County

p. 35, Tuscobia Trail, Barron & Washburn Counties

p. 36, Sand Creek Segment, Polk County

p. 37, top, Canada geese on ice, Barron County; bottom, orange fungi, Tuscobia Trail, Barron County

p. 38, tree felled by beavers, Rusk County

p. 39, Firth Lake boardwalk, near Interpretive Center, New Auburn, Chippewa County

p. 40, Marquette Segment, Northern Columbia County

p. 41, Chippewa Moraine Segment, Chippewa County

p. 42, Lake Holcombe, Chippewa County

p. 43, Monarch butterfly

p. 44, top, chickadee; bottom, bee on petunia, both near Otter Lake, Chippewa County

p. 45, bloodroot, near Devil's Lake, Sauk County

pp. 46-47 top, Chippewa Moraine Segment, near New Auburn, Chippewa County

p. 47, bottom photo, Leopard frog, Taylor County

pp. 48-49, Mondeaux Esker Segment, Taylor County

p. 50, Black Swallowtail butterfly

p. 51, near Mondeaux Flowage, Taylor County; bottom photo, inside of pine stump

pp. 52-54 *Grandfather Falls Segment, Lincoln County

p. 55, Wisconsin River, Grandfather Falls Segment, Lincoln County

p. 58 (*top) - 60, Eau Claire Dells Segment, Marathon County

pp. 61-62, *Plover River Segment, Marathon County

pp. 63-64, *Belmont, Emmons, Hartman Creek Segments, Portage and Waupaca Counties

p. 65, top, McKenzie Creek Segment, Burnett County; bottom, Valley View Segment, Dane County

p. 66, restored prairie, Valley View Segment, Dane County

p. 67, 1,260-foot historic Stewart train tunnel, connecting route, Exeter Crossing Road, Green County

p. 68, top, Wedde Creek Segment, Waushara County

p. 70, Ice fishing, Otter Lake and Chapman Lake, Chippewa County

p. 71, clockwise, from upper left, Mourning Cloak, Yellow Swallowtail, Fritillary, and Monarch butterflies

p. 72, clockwise, from upper left, Monarchs, Red Admiral and Fritillary, and Yellow Sulphur butterflies

p. 73 & 76, *connecting route, Columbia & Sauk Counties, Portage Canal Segment, Northern Columbia County

pp. 74-75, Marquette Segment, Northern Columbia County (this segment is no longer open)

pp. 77-82, Devil's Lake Segment, Sauk County

p. 83, Wattled Crane from South Africa, International Crane Foundation, Necedah

p. 84, Whooping Crane, International Crane Foundation, Necedah

p. 85, Prairie Moraine Park, Dane County

p. 86, Verona Segment, Dane County

pp. 87-88, Lapham Peak Segment, Waukesha County

p. 90, trillium, Glenbeulah Segment, Sheboygan County

p. 91, Chippewa County

p. 92, oak tree, Lodi Marsh Wildlife & Bird Refuge, Lodi Marsh Segment, Dane County

pp. 93-97, Southern Holy Hill Segment, Washington County

p. 98, *Belmont, Emmons, Hartman Creek Segment, Waupaca County

p. 99, clockwise from upper left, mossy rock; Stone Elephant, Blue Spring Lake Segment, Jefferson County; rock bridge, New Wood Segment, Lincoln County; Devil's Lake Segment, Sauk County

p. 100, top, mullein; bottom, Shattuck Lake (a kettle lake), Chippewa Moraine Segment, Chippewa County

p. 101, Devil's Lake State Park, Sauk County

p. 102, Manitowoc, Manitowoc County

p. 103, glass ornament, near Bruce; blue silo, Algoma connecting route, Kewaunee County; pig, near Westfield

p. 105, lawn ornaments from various road walks

p. 106, top, Lake Michigan, Algoma; bottom, connecting route, Kewaunee County

p. 107, *Ahnapee State Trail, Maplewood, Door County

pp. 108-111, *Potawatomi State Park, Sturgeon Bay Segment, Eastern Terminus of the Ice Age Trail, Door County

pp. 112-116, *Holy Hill Segment, Washington County

p. 116, bottom left, *Powder Hill Tower, Pike Lake Segment, Washington County

p. 117, Wood Lake Segment, Taylor County

p. 118, Map of the Ice Age National Scenic Trail, courtesy of the Ice Age Trail Alliance

p. 119, Wattled Crane, International Crane Foundation, Necedah

p. 120-121, Boardwalk, Ridge Run County Park, West Bend Segment, Washington County

p. 122, right, Eau Claire Dells Segment, Marathon County

p. 123, top, Culvert, Clyde Hill Road, connecting route, Kewaunee River State Trail, Kewaunee County; *bottom, "Hillbilly Hilton," Lumber Camp Segment, Langlade County

p. 124, Murphy Flowage, Hemlock Creek Segment, Rusk County